PRAISE FOR *WHEN IT'S FOURTH AND LONG*

"Through Josh's bout with cancer, he was allowed to see the reality of his own mortality. In this book you will read about the lessons he's learned and how God has brought him through that trial to be an ambassador for the Lord Jesus."

AARON KAMPMAN
Green Bay Packers' Pro Bowl defensive lineman

"In life, storms do come, and they come in many different ways. Whether it's literally a hurricane (my family and I lived through the tragedies of Hurricane Katrina) or a battle with cancer, the only solid rock is Christ. Josh's story shows us all how to build a strong foundation."

DANNY WUERFFEL
1996 Heisman Trophy winner

"When I saw how weak Josh's physical body was after surgery and chemotherapy, I realized how strong his faith is. His amazing story spans the low of cancer and the highs of playing in the Pro Bowl and becoming a godly husband and father. It will truly inspire you!"

RYAN LONGWELL
Green Bay Packers' all-time leading scorer

"Josh's disease disabled his body, but it softened his heart. God was at work developing, from the inside out, a long-term player for His kingdom purposes."

JOE URCAVICH
Green Bay Packers' chaplain and
pastor of Green Bay Community Church

"Josh's story demonstrates that living in God's will is not always easy and does not make us impervious to tribulation. But through the many hardships Josh has faced, his Christian walk has consistently brought glory to God."

TROY POLOMALU
Pittsburg Steelers' Pro Bowl safety

When It's Fourth and Long

JOSH BIDWELL

HARVEST HOUSE PUBLISHERS

EUGENE, OREGON

Front and back cover photos © Tampa Bay Buccaneers, National Football League

Cover by Left Coast Design, Portland, Oregon

WHEN IT'S FOURTH AND LONG

Copyright © 2007 by Josh Bidwell
Published by Harvest House Publishers
Eugene, Oregon 97402
www.harvesthousepublishers.com

Library of Congress Cataloging-in-Publication Data
Bidwell, Josh, 1976–
    When it's fourth and long / Josh Bidwell.
        p. cm.
    ISBN-13: 978-0-7369-2052-0
    ISBN-10: 0-7369-2052-8
    1. Bidwell, Josh, 1976- 2. Football players—United States—Biography. I Title.
GV939.B52A3 2007
796.332092—dc22

[B]
                                                                    2007007376

Printed in the United States of America

07 08 09 10 11 12 13 14 15 / VP-SK / 12 11 10 9 8 7 6 5 4 3 2 1

▼

To my beautiful wife, Bethany,
my sons, Brady and Aaron,
and my father, Corey.

ACKNOWLEDGMENTS

▼

I never could have written this book without the help and encouragement I received from many friends and family members. I especially want to thank...

Bob Hawkins Jr. for your gracious invitation to tell my story,

Brett Gilchrist for your creative insights and editing of my manuscript,

Gene Skinner for cleaning it all up for me,

and my Lord and Savior Jesus Christ for being the author of my entire story.

CONTENTS

▼

INTRODUCTION

The entire week had been unbelievable. I regretted that it was almost over; I wanted it to last at least another week. The 2006 Pro Bowl was about to start, so I had about three and a half hours left until the entire experience came to a close. As I sat in the locker room and tried to soak in everything I had experienced, I thought back to the one moment when I fully realized just how special this week had been for me.

I was standing in my Pro Bowl uniform, holding my new son and waiting to take pictures with my wife and my dad, when I realized just how blessed I was to be there. I had played in the NFL long enough to know just how hard it was to make it to that game. I knew that a great season or even a great career wouldn't guarantee that I would ever be a Pro Bowler. Many great NFL players have had long, distinguished careers and were never voted into the Pro Bowl. I appreciated every bit of what being there meant, and I took none of it for granted. I had just enjoyed the best season of my career; I was holding my first child and sharing the entire experience with my closest family. I felt so privileged to be there, or even to be alive.

Standing in that photo session, and then again sitting in the locker room, I could hardly believe that seven years earlier, a doctor's report had not given me much hope. Even today I hear his words in my head as if he had spoken them yesterday.

"Josh, you're done," the doctor had said rather bluntly. The words hung in the air, almost refusing to land. But when they did, they landed with a thud, leaving me in shock. Just a few days earlier, the Green Bay Packers' special-teams coach had told me they had released the other punter and that I had made the team. My lifelong dream of playing in the NFL had come true, and I was flying high.

But now this. To say I was confused and fearful is an understatement; my world was crashing down around me. I had just met this doctor, and suddenly he is telling me I have testicular cancer and is making final pronouncements about my future and maybe my life.

Questions swirled in my head. What did he mean, I was done? Was the cancer beyond cure and my life over? In a desperate attempt to remain calm, I asked the urologist to explain. He replied that four types of cells are associated with this cancer. One is nonagressive, but the other three are very aggressive. The lab's report from my biopsy had taken him by surprise: My tumor contained all four types of cancer cells! This meant without a doubt that my life's goal, which I was finally so close to reaching, was certainly in jeopardy. But more terrifying than that, my life was hanging in the balance.

When I received the news, I was determined to appear stoic in front of my girlfriend. Bethany was sitting beside me and hearing the same crushing news, and I felt I needed to be strong for her. Also, it was no secret to everyone I knew that I was a Christian, and in my ambition to please everyone around me, I felt as if it was my duty to at least appear strong, in control, and unfazed by this devastating news. But only a few minutes later, as Bethany and I walked down the long corridor leading to the player's parking lot, my knees buckled. I slumped to the ground and leaned against the wall sobbing. I was only 23 years old, scared, and confused—how in the world could this have happened to me? I was on a journey unlike anything I had ever known, and I wondered if my life up to that point could possibly have prepared me to handle everything I was facing. Had I grown close enough to God to be able to endure this to the end? I didn't have the answer, but I would soon find out.

◄ 1

THE BEGINNING

Every little boy needs a hero. If he's fortunate, that hero could be his dad.

My dad was always my hero. He worked at a mill just a mile down the road from our house and came home every day covered in sawdust and completely exhausted from working a long, overnight shift. Still, he always found the time and energy for a wrestling match with his little boy. Those were my favorite moments. When I heard him stirring around early in the morning, I could not get out of bed fast enough to run out and see him. I'd climb up on his lap, confident he had been waiting there just for me. And when he relaxed after work with a bowl of popcorn, I was just as sure he intended to share it with me.

Dad and I always had a great relationship. As an adult, I now know just how important a father is to a young boy. When I look back and see how I was stuck to him at all times, I am thankful that he was responsive enough to give me the personal attention I craved.

My sister, Loraine, is six years older than I am, and as kids, we had a lot of fun together. She was a great older sister who played with me a lot. One of our favorite things to play was school. Our shared room was the classroom, she was always the teacher, and I was always her one-student class. I was only four years old or so and could not read or write, and I can't recall exactly what kind of "assignments" she gave me, but I can tell you that I had plenty of work to do regardless. She set up a fun and elaborate system: For good behavior and for every assignment I did well on, I received a little paper token. When I earned enough tokens, she was to buy me a candy bar as my reward. After playing school almost every day and earning hundreds of tokens, I finally began to realize that I was not likely to get any candy bars from Loraine. Still, for some reason, I was undeterred from wanting to earn more. Perhaps I felt it was just too risky to stop earning my candy bar tokens in case she should ever decide to fulfill her end of the bargain. I'm still waiting.

My mom always made sure I was well cared for, and until I was old enough to go to school, she seemed to love having me around all the time to keep her entertained. I was a typical little boy with two interests: playing hard and eating. Whether I was playing in the front yard or next door with all the neighbor kids, every day at lunchtime I heard my mom's loud voice calling, "Joooooshuaaaa, luuuunch!" I could hear my mom's voice from anywhere, and I knew well enough to get home as soon as I could. She always had a sandwich or soup ready for me and would sit down with me or just be in the room to talk to me during lunch.

Mom has often told me the sad story—and her heart seems to break at the memory—of my first day of school. She says she prepared my lunch as always, went to the front porch, and called out, "Joooooshuaaaa, luuuunch!" After a moment, she realized I was not coming home for lunch as usual because I was at school. She tells me she just cried for a while, realizing her little boy was no longer going to be eating lunch with her every day. I can actually remember her telling me that story when I got home after my first day of school. I also remember being surprised that I didn't hear her calling me from the school—she had as loud of a voice as anyone I knew. Mom had a way of always making me laugh. She and I definitely had a special relationship.

I can recall many wonderful times we had as a family. We enjoyed a lot of family outings together, either going to a park on a weekend to play on the playgrounds and hang out with other families for barbecues or following my endless string of soccer games, wrestling matches, track meets, and basketball games. We also attended Loraine's plays or band events.

Every holiday was a big event as well. I have so many great memories of Christmas mornings, getting up early and running out to see the stockings filled and the tree littered with presents. (One year, my dad even dressed up as Santa Claus, which gave me unique insight into the song "I Saw Mommy Kissing Santa Claus.") Then, later in the day, we would gather with other family members at my dear Grandma Cleone's house. Looking back on those years with the perspective I have now, I can easily see that my mom and dad worked very hard to make life as stable and as special as they could for my sister and me. As far as I could tell, we had everything we needed.

Spending all those days at home with my mom, I received my first introduction to God from her. She told me all she knew about Jesus and held me enraptured with stories from the Bible. A large Bible on our mantle had a picture on the cover of Jesus wearing a crown of thorns. Jesus was a real figure in my mind as a child, but I didn't understand what a relationship with Him entailed. I was too young at the time, and the Bible stories I heard entertained me more than they guided my decision making.

We often talked about Jesus at home, and I heard many stories about Him at Sunday school, but I quickly began to have questions about God when I became old enough to see some of the things that were going on within and around my family. We only lived one block from the church my sister and I attended, but Mom and Dad rarely went with us. I don't remember the name of the church, but I do remember that it was a fun place for kids, with great teachers, lots of crafts, and biblical puppet shows that familiarized me with a lot of the events and stories of the Bible. I didn't yet know what being a Christian meant, but I went to church because that was what I was supposed to do and because I enjoyed the fun classes. However, even at a young age and even though I had a lot of fun, I was aware enough to wonder, if church was so important and God was so real, why did Mom and Dad drop off my sister and me rather than come with us?

To this day, my mom is one of the sweetest women I know. She has a soft, kind spirit and a very caring heart. However, she has been in a huge struggle with drugs and alcohol virtually her entire adult life. Her addiction began early in her teen years as a way for her to cope with breakdowns in her family. Addictions like these do not go away easily, and they affect everyone around you. Mom was careful to keep me as far away from that part of her life as she could, but drug and alcohol abuse is not something that is easily hidden or controlled. I did get glimpses of her turmoil from time to time, and it sometimes led to arguments between her and my dad that were impossible to keep hidden from my sister and me. These fights were never physical, but they included words that hurt just the same.

Many times I saw my mom crying and in emotional pain after Dad would have to leave the room or the house for a while, and my heart always broke to see her hurting so much. Mom tells me today that one of the bright spots in those dark days was seeing her pale, skinny little boy, usually with a huge red afro, walk out of his room, crawl up on her lap, give her a big long hug, and tell her over and over that everything would be all right. I knew those moments made her feel better, and I felt great too, as if I were in some way helping to fix whatever problem she and Dad were going through.

And then, before I knew it, Mom and Dad were no longer together. Seemingly overnight, we were all moving out of the only house I had ever known. Loraine was 14, and in her anger over our parents' breakup, began running away from home. She was also beginning her own long, gripping journey down the road of alcoholism and drug addictions. My family was splitting up and moving apart from one another, and I wouldn't spend quality time with my sister for almost two decades. But God is so amazing and faithful. Loraine is 36 now with an 18-year-old son, Corey, and a 4-year-old daughter, Kendra. Loraine eventually gave her life to Christ and has been freed, by the grace of God, from her alcoholism and drug addictions. However, it was not without a lot of hard work on her part, and I will always admire her for that. She suffered through times that I could never imagine experiencing, and I am filled with joy to see her loving the Lord and working so hard to stay strong against those past addictions and to be a great mom for her two children. When I see her today, I thank God for protecting her during some of the most terrible situations anyone could ever face. I'm grateful He brought my big sister back into my life safe and sound.

The months following my parents' divorce were very difficult for me. I was too young at the time to understand what was going on. I didn't know where one parent was when I was with the other. I was having a hard time feeling safe and secure. I was at Dad's house on some days and at Mom's house on others. I was enrolled in three grade schools in one year as I moved back and forth between living with my mom and my dad. This lasted about a year until the custody situation between my parents was resolved. I was afraid of living with one parent and never seeing the other again. Moving back and forth between Mom's and Dad's, I sometimes wondered if they were fighting over who had to take care of me rather than who wanted to take care of me. I felt at times that when one parent dropped me off at the other's house, that parent was finally getting some free time away from the burden of taking care of me and that maybe I would never see him or her again. I always made sure to give them big hugs and tell them I loved them just to make sure they would come back for me.

As I look back on those days, I realize my parents never did anything to make me feel that way. But being so young and so confused, I simply feared the worst. The uncertainty made me a very self-reflective, introverted child at too young of an age. I had a lot of childhood confusion and confidence issues because so much seemed to be going wrong and so much was out of my control. I had terrible thoughts: What if my parents don't want me anymore? I started to wonder what I may have done to cause everything that was happening. My confusion later turned into anger.

I remember contemplating serious matters that a young boy should not have to worry about: What was my relationship to the new people who were appearing in my families' lives? How could I fit in at a new school when I kept switching all the time? Whom would I live with? How long would I be there? How much would I see the other parent? I also wondered where my sister was and if I would ever see her again.

I thought about God a lot too. I recalled the stories of His strength, love, protection, and care that Mom told me. I remember wondering, if these things were really true about God, why was He not fixing the mess my family and I were in? I never questioned whether God was real; I always knew He was. I just did not understand what His role was in our lives and why He was not fixing my family's problems. I also wondered how my mom could tell me so much about His power in our lives but not experience that power in her struggles. These questions and many more would remain unanswered for a long time.

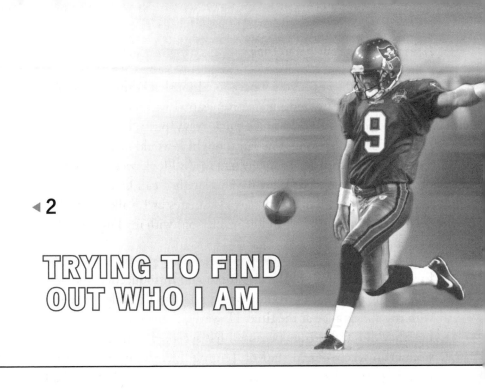

2

TRYING TO FIND OUT WHO I AM

As my familiar world was crumbling away, a new world began to take shape. My father remarried soon after these events took place, and he and I, with my new stepmother and stepbrother, moved to the tiny country community of Tenmile, Oregon, to begin a new chapter in our lives. I was only nine years old when suddenly my old life disappeared and a new one began, and the changes kept me guessing as I tried to figure out who I truly was.

If you ever have had to start at a new school, especially halfway through the school year, you know how difficult and uncomfortable it can be. I was enrolled in Tenmile Elementary School in the middle of my fourth-grade year. I can still remember my first day at school. My dad took me to the front office to fill out some paperwork. He introduced me to the few people working in the tiny office, including the principal. They in turn took me just outside the door to a neighboring room that was to be my classroom for the remainder of the year. Now, I have to admit that at this time in my life, I was not in my most attractive years. I was the palest person around with a few freckles and a thick, wavy, puffy, bright red head of hair. For some reason, my dad thought it would be funny never to cut my hair until he absolutely had to! As I look back on pictures of myself in those days, I just have to laugh. I can imagine what I must have looked like to my new classmates as I walked into Mr. Sevdy's classroom (in the middle of a lesson) with my huge red afro swaying from side to side.

I was led to the front of the classroom and introduced as the new kid joining the class. I certainly wasn't going to fly under the radar with my appearance at the time. However, if any kids made fun of me, they did it in private because I felt accepted immediately. The wonderful teachers and staff of Tenmile Elementary will always have a special place in my heart. They made me feel as if I had lived in their community and attended their school my entire life. Making the transition even better, all of the other kids were great as well. They accepted me right away, and I had a ton of friends in no time. I still have many close friends today who were in that classroom the day I arrived.

Even though I was made to feel fairly comfortable in my new environment, I was still very confused as to who I was, or more specifically, who I wanted to be. Not someday as a grown up, but right then and there. How did I fit in with those around me? What was my niche? How was I unique, and what would set me apart and define to others who I was? I didn't feel as if I had much to offer when I first arrived in Tenmile, so my search for an identity took me to the fields of competition. There I could establish an identity, and there I could also vent a lot of the anger that I had.

Being such a young boy, I was not yet able to deal with the confusion in my past and some friction in my new relationships. I became angry, and I used my anger to develop an aggressive, competitive attitude on the field. Playing well and winning made me feel great, and those experiences helped me escape from the anger and frustration festering inside me. Fortunately, though, anger was not my only source of motivation. I truly loved sports and had a lot of fun out there. I may have been way too intense at times, but I was also simply having a great time.

In his book *Bringing Up Boys,* Dr. James Dobson offers helpful insights into young boys and their need for competition. He demonstrates that competition can help boys find their manhood as they grow and develop. Reading his observations, I could not help but look back and see exactly what I was thinking at this time in my life. I loved to compete! I loved to win! I didn't crave making people feel bad by beating them in whatever we were competing in, but I loved the way victory made me feel. Whether in school, on the sports field, or in silly games my friends and I played, I loved to compete, and that was all that mattered to me. Competition is healthy for both young girls and young boys, but boys usually get a little extra out of it, as they are more likely to want to compete in everything all the time.

I've had a passion for sports for as long as I remember. Even before I was in school, I was eager to sign up for any sport that I could play. My dad did a great job of recognizing my love for sports and working hard to encourage my passion. He signed me up for every sport he could think of. During my elementary years I competed in football, baseball, basketball, track, wrestling, and soccer. I don't remember ever asking my dad to sign me up for all of these sports, and never once did he make me play a sport I didn't want to play.

But every time he came home and told me that wrestling was about to start, or my first basketball practice at the YMCA was coming, I would get so excited. I wanted to play everything, and he always found out what sport was happening at the time and signed me up right away. I felt as if I was getting a gift when he came home from work and told me I was on a soccer team that was starting the next day. He got so much joy out of seeing me have fun and compete, and I loved that he never once made me feel any pressure on the court or field. He just stood on the sidelines, grinning ear to ear every time we made eye contact and never saying a word to me that was not one of encouragement. I guess I just took for granted that Dad would know what I wanted to play and do what needed to be done to get me out there—which was exactly what he did.

My years at Tenmile Elementary were good ones. There I met my new best friends, Brian and Kevin Tommasini, who would play huge roles in my spiritual life growing up and would become two of the best friends I could ever have. Brian and I are the same age, and Kevin is one year older. Brian and Kevin's parents, Frank and Marge Tommasini, taught me life lessons and showed me the type of hospitality that I still try to emulate as I interact with others today. I love them dearly. Kevin and Brian were two of Frank and Marge's seven children, and I have grown very close to all of them.

Frank was our coach for a number of sports when we were kids, and in his no-nonsense way, he taught me how to work hard on the field to get the most out of myself. Marge is quite possibly the sweetest woman I have ever met. She treated every one of the kids' friends as if they were family—especially me because I spent almost as much time at their house as they did. She never once complained about all the mooching I did, from eating their food to bumming rides almost every day. Even with seven of her own children, she always found time to make room for one more. Knowing she was there if I ever needed her made the world a better place for me.

Brian and Kevin were homeschooled in their elementary years, so the only time I saw them was after school, either at our practices, at games, or when I went over to their house to play. However, because we lived in the country and didn't have a lot of neighbors to play with, I spent most of my weekends at their house doing what boys do best—playing and getting dirty. We played basketball, football, and wiffleball, had creek wars (standing waist deep in our creek while hunting for each other as the enemy), and still found the time and daylight to play cops and robbers on our bikes up in their forest, where we carved out a ton of trails. All this would happen in the course of one day; we were very efficient and took our recreation extremely seriously.

I was always welcome at the Tommasini home, but especially when Kevin and Brian had a major chore to do. They would actually call me up and ask me to come over to play, but after riding the three long miles to their house, I would find out they just wanted me to help them with whatever major project their parents assigned them. For a ten-year-old, three miles felt like thirty, especially riding a BMX bike over two pretty big hills. When I finally got to their house and found out what they were up to, I knew helping them out would be less work than riding back home again. I was stuck, and we all knew that the faster we got their chores done, the sooner we would be free to play. Still, Kevin and Brian were the best friends I could have asked for.

Kevin and Brian were just as competitive as I was. Having two great friends who always wanted to practice and play as much as I did made my athletic experiences even better. Even though Kevin and Brian were both homeschooled, they played for our elementary school's athletic teams. Without those sports, we may never have become friends, and they certainly would not have had as much of an impact on me as they did. I noticed their character and intensity right away and tried to emulate them as best I could. But it would not be until a few years later that I would find myself searching hard for the power in my life that Kevin, Brian, and their entire family had in theirs. Little did I know at that time that athletics was only a small part of who they all really were.

I am a firm believer that athletics can be an incredibly valuable tool to help kids develop confidence and a strong work ethic. That's what happened for me right from the start. However, there was one sport that I wondered if I should play again, and that was baseball. Before I moved to Tenmile, I played in a youth league that was similar to T-ball, but the players actually pitched to the hitters. In this league, if the pitcher walked the hitter, rather than the hitter going to first base, he was given a chance to hit the ball off the tee instead. I was about eight years old at the time, and you can probably imagine that not too many eight-year-olds can throw a lot of consistent strikes. For me though, it came pretty easily. I was a head taller than all the other kids, and I was blessed with a pretty strong and fairly accurate arm, so I ended up doing pretty well. I began my baseball career thinking I would love playing baseball.

That optimism faded the following season, and it was a real gut check for me to see just how mentally tough I could be. My first season of baseball at my new grade school in Tenmile was during my fourth-grade year. The league was set up with two different levels—the majors and the minors. Fourth graders weren't likely to be chosen for the majors, but somehow I made the cut. Frank was the coach of the majors team, the Tenmile Blue Jays, and he saw some talent in me based on my size and athletic ability, so he chose me to stay on the majors that year. We probably played 15 or 20 games that season, and I always started as the center fielder. But incredibly, I did not get a single hit! Not one! I don't recall even fouling one off, though the law of averages suggests I should have done at least that at some point. I played in every single game, and I stood at bat in every single game, but I never got that coveted hit.

I used to daydream that summer, out in the field in front of our house, about just closing my eyes and connecting with a fastball for the longest home run in Blue Jays history. I hated my terrible streak, but the only thing that stopped it was the end of the season. It was horrible.

Still, I had a lot of fun. Defensively, I had done really well. I was able to throw the ball all the way from center field to the catcher at home, which not a lot of kids that age were able to do, and I was fast enough and coordinated enough to run down a fly ball and sometimes make the difficult catch. I was just not a good hitter, and I really don't know why.

I sometimes wonder why Frank kept me in the lineup the entire season when I was obviously useless with a bat in my hands. I can only guess that he wanted to teach me about perseverance and not giving up on myself. He refused to give up on me, and he probably expected me to follow suit as I took the batter's box on game day.

But I wanted to quit. I remember riding home with my dad when the season was over and telling him I didn't want to play baseball anymore. I'm sure he wasn't too surprised, but he suggested I wait until the next summer and make my decision then.

By the time the next season came, I was even bigger and faster than before, and I had regained the confidence that I could be a decent baseball player if I kept working hard at it. That is exactly what I did, and my efforts paid off beautifully. My batting average that season was over .500, and I even hit a few home runs. The difference from the season before was like night and day. I went from being the worst hitter on the team to being one of the best. I'm thankful today that Frank taught me not to quit, and even more thankful that my dad gave me just the right words of encouragement when I was considering giving up. Baseball would eventually become one of my best sports.

I was always one of the bigger and faster kids in my class, so I was able to excel in all the sports I signed up for. I made friends very quickly with my teammates and soon began to establish my self-identity in sports. The success I began enjoying quickly became my escape. I liked hearing compliments from other kids and parents about my performance. In fact, I started relying on them. I wanted to be the nice guy everyone liked and to be the best at whatever I did. The approval I received made me feel important.

This was a powerful motivator. For the next few years I struggled with the ebbs and flows of my performance and the emotions that came with winning and losing. To play poorly and lose a game was the worst scenario I could possibly imagine. As I grappled with that, I was also devastated if others thought poorly of me. If I were not to play well, or if my team did not win a game, I was sure everyone blamed me. I felt as though I let everyone down, and I had no idea how to deal with that disappointment.

This went on for the rest of my elementary years. Life experiences provide us with constant reminders that we can never please everyone, but still I was on a mission to be a people pleaser. Whenever I discovered that someone didn't like me, I had no idea how to deal with the rejection.

One day, I was with my dad and some friends at our local pizza parlor. It was a bit crowded and noisy, so I really couldn't hear anything clearly that was outside our conversation at the table—that is, until I heard my name spoken from the table just behind me. What I heard next absolutely crushed me. As I focused in on the subject of their conversation, I heard the aunt of a good friend of mine completely tearing me apart. She was freely sharing her opinion that I was one of the cockiest kids in the area and that all I cared about was being the star. She felt that whatever sport I was playing in, the only reason for my success was that I was a ball hog and that I made sure no one else on my team could have success.

She went on to attack every area of my life to prove her perception of who I was.

As I sat there and listened to this conversation behind me, I was absolutely crushed. My efforts to please everyone had obviously fallen short, and I was devastated. Those words plagued me throughout my high school years. I wanted to be successful in sports, but I would do whatever I could to ease off a bit on the court or the field, trying to make sure I didn't appear to be a selfish, arrogant person. Living in the fear of others' perception of me left me ruined at times and kept me from being as successful as I could have been and from enjoying myself more growing up.

The contrast between the encouraging words I heard from my coaches and my dad and the destructive words I heard from my friend's aunt could not have been greater. I wouldn't learn how to balance these mixed messages for a long time.

3

WHICH ROAD TO CHOOSE

Our tiny community of Tenmile didn't have a middle school or high school, so in my sixth-grade year, I began commuting about ten miles to the town of Winston. That school year ended with a bit of a scare. My teacher, Mrs. Wilkerson, called a meeting with my dad and me. She told my dad that my grades were on the line and that I was dangerously close to being held back. I was terrified.

That year especially, I had a hard time trying to figure out not only who I was but also who I wanted to be. I decided to hang out with a few kids who I thought were cool but who were very defiant and disruptive in class. I spent that year just trying to get by. I still haven't finished the report on Egypt I was supposed to have done about 18 years ago. I had become lazy and uninterested in class. I was convinced that being cool was more important than learning and being accountable to my parents and teachers.

But as I listened to Mrs. Wilkerson tell my dad I should be held back for one more year of sixth grade, she definitely had all of my attention. However, she told my dad she was certain I had learned far more that year than my grades reflected and that she was sure my problem was not my ability to learn but simply my attitude. She told my dad I was going to be in pretty big trouble if I didn't take my schoolwork more seriously in the years to come.

You can imagine what that ride home was like! I could have cut the tension with a knife. My dad was not a screamer; he was not the type of person to pull the car over, find the biggest stick with the biggest thorns, and whale away on my behind. He was fairly calm when disciplining me. His personality was exactly what my fragile psyche needed. As I mentioned earlier, my dad had always been my hero, the person that I looked up to more than any other. This ride home would change my life forever.

The car was silent as we began the drive home through the Olalla countryside. At about mile three, my dad asked me an unexpected question: "Josh, what do you want to be when you grow up?"

That took me off guard. I was half expecting him to ask me how I should be punished. I was taken aback by his question because he already knew the answer.

"An NFL player."

To a kid in grade school, life is all about dreams with not much perspective on reality. My dad knew that getting to the NFL would be nearly impossible simply because of the competition. He knew my education was the most important thing I had going for me, that I was in danger of wasting an opportunity, and that my choices would affect me for the rest of my life. He told me very calmly that if I didn't get good grades in high school, I could never get to the NFL.

High school? I thought to myself. *What are you talking about? I'm only going into seventh grade!*

As if replying to my unspoken thoughts, he said, "You know, Josh, if you don't learn how to do well in school now, if you don't develop good study habits in these next two years of middle school, you won't be able to do well when you get into high school, where the classes will be much harder. And if you don't get good grades in high school, you won't be able to go to college, and no NFL teams hire guys who have never been to college."

I sat there silent, hearing every word my dad said, and each one really scared me. I wanted to go to the NFL more than anything at that point. I understood clearly what my dad was saying, and I was suddenly afraid that maybe I would never be able to do well in school. School was already pretty hard for me anyway, and I wondered if working harder would really have any effect on my grades. I never thought I was very smart, and now I was being weighed down with the possibility that I might not be able to figure school out, which would lead to poor grades, no scholarship offers to colleges, and the end of my football dream. It was a hard talk to hear on that drive home.

My dad was the person I looked up to more than anyone. He had always been my best friend, and I knew that he was always very proud of me. The words he said next absolutely crushed me, but they would also end up motivating me to do what I needed to do to make him proud and to reach my goals. "Josh, I am very disappointed in you. You've really let me down."

Making my dad proud had been my goal for as long as I could remember. To hear him say that to me absolutely floored me inside. I had let down the very person I most wanted to be proud of me. I don't suppose my dad could have imagined that as a 12-year-old boy, I was mature enough to have been impacted so powerfully by the short conversation we had that day. The conversation was over when we got home, and life went on as normal, but I was changed forever.

As I moved into seventh grade, the schoolwork got harder, and the teachers were far more demanding. I had a few questions in my mind: *Can I do this? Am I smart enough? Can I learn good study habits, and do I have what it takes to learn and get great grades?* I really didn't feel as if I had it in me, but I began working as hard as I could. I soon discovered the answers to all those fears I had. My very first quarterly report card as a student at Winston Middle School was filled entirely with A's. I will never forget how great that felt—I was genuinely shocked! I had worked hard and completed all of my assignments, but I was not thoroughly convinced that I was a smart kid. That insecurity disappeared when that first report card arrived. I remember feeling as if I were in a different league after that; I was one of the smart kids! Not everyone got all A's that report card, but a few of us did. I wasn't always a straight-A student, but nothing lower than a B would ever show up on my grade reports again. That report card was the springboard to developing the confidence in myself I would need to reach my dreams.

My athletic success carried on into middle school as well. I was the quarterback of a great football team. We were undefeated our eighth-grade year—a first in our school's history. We had one of the best basketball teams in the area and had just as much success in soccer, track, and baseball. My success continued to drive me, and I put a huge amount of pressure on myself, expecting perfection at all times.

Of course, I would never achieve perfection, and even though I enjoyed great personal success and played on some very good teams, I never felt enough satisfaction to relax and enjoy the moment in those great times. Success motivated me to continue to work hard so I could achieve it again. Failure pushed me to work even harder. I had fun and was excited when I did well and the team had success, but that only fed into my drive all the more and pushed me to achieve even greater success, often at a pace I had no way of maintaining.

That lack of fulfillment often left me heartbroken and lonely because no one really seemed to understand. No one seemed to know how to help me relax and slow down a bit, so I drove myself to be the most successful person I could be. Whether in school or in competition, I was determined to be the best. I thought success would validate who I was to others and to myself. What a fragile state I was in! I thank the Lord that He was protecting me, even from myself, as I struggled to find out who I was.

Other than my introduction to God from my mom, it would not be until our move to Tenmile that I would develop relationships with people who were Christians and who would begin to show me clearly the reality of God in their lives and words. Deep inside me during those years in elementary school, middle school, and high school, I thought of God often. I often asked myself how He fit into my life and how could I know I was going to heaven when I died. These questions became more important to me the older I got.

When I first met the Tommasini family back in elementary school, I quickly discovered they were Christians. They were good people who never did any of the stuff I had seen a lot of other people do. But more than that, they always talked about God as if He lived right there in their house. He was a part of the family. In fact, He was the leader of the family. They spoke of Jesus as if He was the one making things happen; decisions were made because of His direction, and things happened because He wanted them to.

I was only in fourth grade when I first met the Tommasinis, so I didn't pick up on the fact that Jesus wanted to know me in a personal way. I saw the way they acted, and I resolved to do the same things they did, thinking that by acting in a good manner, I might prove my worth to God. By the time Kevin, Brian, and I were in middle school, their days of homeschool were done, and I got a chance to see them in action at school.

By this time, I started wanting some kind of eternal security. I wanted to know I was going to heaven. But how could I know for sure? What did I need to do to make sure I knew God in the right way and to be confident I was going to be in heaven when I died? I spent a lot of time with the Tommasinis and saw that they seemed to be sure of what I was so unsure of, so I decided to try to do exactly what Brian and Kevin did. They worked hard in school, they were great players in whatever sport we were playing, and they were both very well liked by everyone because they were such nice kids and never got into trouble. I spent a lot of time trying to make sure everyone liked me, so it made perfect sense to me to simply emulate everything they did or did not do. I convinced myself that by doing all the right things, I could be sure I was going to heaven. After all, I could see that Kevin, Brian, and their family knew of their eternal security and were at peace in their relationships with God, so I felt I could have that too as long as I was on the straight and narrow.

One day in seventh grade, I saw something that still to this day challenges me to step up and be a leader among my peers. The students were all at lunch. Some were in the cafeteria, others were in the gym, and most of us were out on the track, which surrounded the football field. In the distance, I saw a group of boys putting one poor kid into an outhouse that was just off the track and sitting near the edge of a pretty big ditch. Their brilliant idea was to lock him in while they pushed it over into the ditch. Before I knew it and before the pranksters were successful, Kevin ran over and rescued the young boy from this terrible predicament.

That was a moment I will never forget. I learned at that moment that protecting a person's integrity is more important than going along with the crowd regardless of how funny or cool their actions seem at the time. Kevin knew that what they were doing was wrong and that it was up to him to do something about it. He knew that the prank would probably get a laugh and that he could have just as easily helped out in the joke. But he didn't. He took a stand to stay true to himself and to God by doing what he knew was right when it needed to be done. That event made me all the more determined to be the same type of person—a godly man who is confident and always takes a stand for what is right regardless of the cost. I wanted to be a young man of integrity.

The Bible teaches us in Hebrews 11:6 that "without faith it is impossible to please God." Jesus Himself tells us in John 15:5 that we can do nothing apart from Him. It did not take much for me to see the truth in those two Scriptures. Regardless of how hard I tried, I could not live up to the standard I saw Kevin and Brian living up to. They weren't perfect, and they had their own times of mistakes and failures, but those were much fewer than mine. Kevin and Brian had a strength in dealing with those times that I was unable to emulate. They had a peace and a purpose in their lives that obviously superseded their academic and athletic endeavors and defined them on a deeper level. They never seemed to be concerned with what others thought of them but were always trying simply to be the best they could be for themselves. Why were they so sure of their relationship with God, and what did I need to do to have that in my own life?

By my eighth-grade year I was becoming desperate. I was trying to read the Bible on my own and with Brian, but I didn't feel as if I understood any of it. I was praying, staying out of trouble, and getting good grades. I was hearing good things from others about how liked I was and what a good kid I had been. What else did I need to do?

During that summer, while visiting my Grandpa Stan and new Grandma Beverly, I had a chance to go to church a few times. My grandfather recently had been remarried to an amazing woman whom I consider to be a godsend to my grandfather and to our whole family. Grandma Bev loves the Lord with all her heart. She has an amazing spirit about her and a passion for God that I dearly wanted to have. One evening, she and I began to talk about our lives and about God, and she recognized all the signs of a broken young boy who was desperate to have a relationship with God. She could see the turmoil I was experiencing and knew what I needed.

"Josh, this Sunday at church, the pastor will baptize anyone who wants to give his life to Jesus. If that's what you want to do, just let me know, and you can go to church with your grandpa and me."

Oh man, I was so excited. I had just been to a wonderful event at a local church the night before, where an excellent speaker challenged us young kids to see that being cool apart from God was not cool at all. He convinced me that my life was filled with empty ambitions and things that were pulling me away from God. After getting so excited about God that night and talking with Grandma Bev the next day, I was ready. I wanted to know I was going to heaven.

I remember wondering, *What are the odds that the very Sunday I want to become a Christian, this church just happens to be having baptisms?* Little did I know until years later that this church baptized people after every Sunday service in the summers. The church was Applegate Christian Fellowship, just outside of the neighboring southern Oregon town of Jacksonville. Jon Courson, formerly the senior pastor and now one of three teaching pastors at Applegate, is an amazing preacher. After his sermon that Sunday, I rushed down to the "hot tub," which was not very warm, and stood in the water as pastor Jon asked me questions about my understanding of what I was doing. I accepted what he was saying and agreed that this was exactly what I wanted to do. And so, with my mom, Grandma Bev, Grandpa Stan, and the entire remaining congregation looking on, I was baptized that day during the summer of my eighth-grade year.

At the time, I thought the act of being baptized was what I needed to do to get to heaven. When I went back home after that visit to see my mom and family, my decision to get baptized was met with some disdain by some people in my family. I still am not sure why, but some family members grilled me about the decision I had made.

"Do you really know what you've done? Now you have to live every day for God. Do you think you can do that? Now you have to be one of those Christians who only does things for God."

That terrified me. I didn't understand why they were so mad or what they were saying. I wondered if I had made the right choice. What if I didn't live up to God's expectations? I just wanted to know I was going to heaven, but suddenly I was hearing that being baptized was not enough. Now I had to be a fanatical Christian who couldn't do anything but go to church and read the Bible. I didn't want to give up on my dreams. I was afraid my life would change for the worse now that I had been baptized. On the one hand, I was excited because I felt I did what I was supposed to do to get to heaven by physically being dunked in some water at a church. But on the other hand, I was worried that I would not be able to or didn't want to become the person I was being told I had to be.

I had been excited about making the right choice, but now I had more questions than answers.

AM I CERTAIN?

The talk my dad had given me in our truck on the way home from my sixth-grade parent-teacher conference had changed me. I had gone on to earn great grades in middle school, to become successful in sports, and to make a lot of friends. I had learned how to study and felt prepared to move on to harder classes in high school. My confidence was building as I took each step closer toward my dream of playing in the NFL.

But I wasn't so confident about my relationship with God, and the growing uncertainty was difficult for me to handle. Was I saved? Was I going to heaven? I simply was not sure. I felt as if I had a chance—I'd been baptized, after all—but was that what I was supposed to do to get to heaven? I was filled with doubts.

That would all change, by God's grace, on a Sunday morning during my second year of high school. I had spent an entire Saturday at Kevin and Brian's house playing hard and getting dirty. We did it all, as was our custom. We played basketball on lowered rims so we could do our best Michael Jordan imitations. We played home run derby on our custom wiffleball field, and we were up in the forest, chasing each other around on bikes. Brian's bike had no tire on its back wheel, but he kept riding around at top speed on just a rim, even hitting a big jump we built on one of the trails. How did he not kill himself? As the day came to a close and the light began to fade, I had neither the energy nor the desire to ride my bike the three miles up and over two hills to get back to my house. I called my dad and asked if I could stay the night with the Tommasinis and come home the next day. Of course, he said yes.

That next morning, as the family was getting showered and ready for church, I just hung around, waiting for a ride home. All ten of us piled into their Dodge Caravan, and the plan was for them to drop me off on their way to church. I certainly couldn't visit their church that day—I was wearing the same clothes I had worn during the entire previous day's activities (slightly discolored at that point, of course). I was dirty and stinky! But as we approached my driveway, there was no slowing down and we raced right past.

Frank Tommasini was a somewhat short, very muscular man who could be extremely intimidating. He had been a power lifter when he was younger, and he told us that at one point, he had long hair and looked just like a professional wrestler. By his own admission, he did not know God during those years and spent his time doing whatever he wanted, heading down a path he had no business being on. Later in his life, he gave himself fully to God, and God took care of the mess he had made of his life and made him into the passionate man of God he still is today. At this point he was still pretty big and strong, but in a normal, non-drug-aided way. Frank had a very raspy voice that he lost years ago. I liked to think his muscles got so big they squished his vocal cords beyond recovery, but I'm not sure that was the reason.

So there I sat, smelly, dirty, and on my way to church. Just in case he had simply forgotten, I raised my hand in the back of the van to get his attention and said in a quiet voice, "Uh, Frank, you forgot to stop and drop me off."

"No I didn't, Bids," he said. "You're going to church with us today."

What? No one had informed me of this. I said to him, "But Frank, I'm not dressed for church. I'm all dirty."

Frank then said something that actually made me feel pretty good at the time. "Don't worry, Bids. God doesn't care what you look like."

That did make me feel a little better for a second. Then it hit me. "Uh, Frank," I said, "what about everyone else at church?" I'm sure if the roles were reversed, I would probably go out of my way to steer clear of a smelly, dirty kid.

"Don't worry about them," he replied. "You're going to church to see what God thinks about you, not everyone else."

Surprisingly, hearing him say that made me feel a lot better. After those words, the conversation was over, and the decision was made. I was going to church whether I wanted to or not.

We soon arrived at the small country church, just a half mile away from my old grade school. Only about 50 people attended this church, but it was so small, it couldn't have held many more than that anyway. When we got there, Kevin, Brian, and I went straight to a small room, where the kids our age had a Sunday school class. This was my first time at this church, but when I went into the room, I instantly felt comfortable. I knew everyone in the room. In fact, every single kid in the room was a good friend of mine. It was great! I didn't feel embarrassed to be there because all these kids were well-liked kids in our school. They were obviously happy to see me there and made me feel right at home.

Our Sunday school teacher, Christa Shigley, was the only person in the room I had never met. I was introduced to her before class began and, as happens in small towns, she said she knew of me and was happy I was there that day. She started the class by getting right to the point of that day's lesson.

"I'm going to ask you a question that I want you to think about silently for a second and then answer to yourself: If you were to die today, how sure are you that you would go to heaven?"

Wow—that was *the* question I had wondered about for so long! Christa encouraged us to try to come up with a percentage in our minds to answer that question. For the next few moments, I took inventory around the room, comparing my life and actions to the others who were there. As I scanned the room, I saw a few people I felt I could stack up well against. I never got in trouble. I was a good student. I was a trustworthy, fairly honest person, and others could count on me for almost anything. In my mind, because of all of my good works and the fact that I truly wanted God to be happy with me, I felt as though I had about an 80-percent chance of getting in. After all, God must have seen that I had wanted to know Him and make Him happy for a few years, so surely my efforts to be a good person were impressive enough to get me to heaven.

After we had a few moments of silent reflection, Christa continued with her lesson. "Do you know that you only have a 100-percent chance or 0-percent chance to get to heaven?"

That got my complete attention. How in the world could I have 100-percent surety and finally know without a doubt that I was going to heaven when I died? She went on to explain the answer to that very question and more. Her words showed me the reason for all the inner turmoil I had endured the past few years. She told us that because of the sin in every person's life, we could do nothing on our own to get to heaven. She referred to Hebrews 11:6—"Without faith it is impossible to please God." She said that meant we couldn't possibly be good enough or do enough on our own to get to heaven. Our innate sin, which goes all the way back to Adam and Eve, causes the gap separating us from God. It is as if we are on one side of the Grand Canyon and God is on the other. We need a bridge to connect us to God, a bridge that only God can provide so we can have a personal relationship with Him again.

Christa then told us that the Bible states clearly that to get to heaven, we need to accept Jesus Christ as our Lord and Savior. She said that we need to pray a simple prayer to God and believe it with all our heart. She encouraged us to pray silently with her as she prayed the most important prayer I have ever prayed.

"Dear Lord Jesus, I am a sinner, and I need You. Thank You for dying on the cross for my sins. I give You my life and ask You to be my Savior and Lord. Thank You for forgiving my sins and giving me eternal life. Take control of my life and make me the person You want me to be."

By doing this we were submitting our lives to God and admitting to Him that we needed His grace in our lives because we were ultimately helpless without Him. God provided the bridge for us to cross so we could have fellowship with Him again. That bridge is the cross of Jesus Christ.

I was so excited to pray that prayer with her that day. After closing the prayer she said that if we had prayed that prayer, we had just become Christians. From that day on, we could know without a doubt that we would spend eternity in heaven with God.

I was elated. For so long I had tried to do whatever I could to have a relationship with God, and it never seemed to work out. I was always under the assumption that I had to do the right things to earn my way to God. I would do something stupid time and time again, and regardless of how hard I tried, I could not seem to reach that point of strength and peace that so many people in my life seemed to have. But everything changed that Sunday morning. I finally knew without a doubt that I was going to heaven, and all I had to do was ask God to save me because I couldn't possibly save myself.

Christa told all of us at the end of the lesson that if we had prayed that prayer with her, we needed to tell someone about it. We needed to find another Christian and tell him or her that we had just prayed to receive Christ so that others could know and help us grow in our relationship with Him. At the end of class, I went right up to her and told her that I prayed just then, and I thanked her deeply for showing me how easy it was to give my life to Jesus. She became an invaluable supporter of my walk with the Lord. She and her husband, Bob, often hosted our Sunday school class and our friends at their house for Bible studies and events, and they are still serving others faithfully to this day.

For the rest of that year and the two remaining years of high school, I was a different person. I had always tried to be on the straight and narrow, never getting into trouble, always being the nice guy whom others could admire and depend on, so on the surface, others might not have seen much of a change. But after giving my life to Christ, I had a new motivation, a new power behind my actions. The Bible tells me that from the moment I prayed to receive Jesus as my Lord and Savior, I was a new creation, a new person completely. There were no fireworks, there was no beam of light from heaven or a loud, booming voice from above announcing the decision that I had made. But I instantly sensed a peace in my heart that I never had before. I would spend the next few years on a journey to find out just whom I had become and who God wanted me to be. For so long, I had been trying to be the person I thought I was supposed to be, and now that I had given my life to God and had seen that His Word tells me He is creating me into a new person, I needed guidance.

One of the most important people in my spiritual growth for those last years of high school, aside from Christa and the Tommasini family, was my English teacher and football coach, Rick Taylor. Mr. Taylor is undoubtedly one of the most passionate Christians I have ever met. For a high school teacher and coach to be such an influence in my Christian walk may seem strange because of today's politically correct separation of church and state. But Mr. Taylor's influence in my life exceeded his role as a teacher and coach. He was an active member of our church. His two sons and two stepdaughters were in my Sunday school class, and his wife was just as passionate about Christ as he was. He was, by all standards, a role model for me. When I was a freshman, Mr. Taylor had enough confidence in me to play me on the varsity team on defense and the kicking positions. Even before I gave my life to Christ, he made an impression on me that would become clearer as time went on. His qualities set him apart from most head football coaches.

He did not have an ounce of arrogance in him. In my experience, most coaches have a swagger about them that comes across as egotistical or pompous. He was a confident coach and had a great football mind for the Xs and Os of the game, but a greater purpose drove his interactions with us and the other coaches.

He never swore. Not one bad word during practice, no uncontrolled outburst of profanity during the halftime speeches of games. He obviously took pains *not* to swear under any circumstances. His understanding of God's instruction and his personal conviction as he walked with the Lord was that no foul language should come from his lips. This was an extremely powerful witness to me. It showed me that Mr. Taylor was mindful of his walk with God *at all times*. He did not put it on hold just because he was running a practice, or making a powerful point in the heat of battle during a game. Letting an obscenity fly here or there would have been much easier for him, and it certainly would have gotten my attention. But that never happened, and believe me, he did not need profanity to get his point across to my teammates and me when we were messing up on the field. His tight rein on his tongue did not earn him anything from God, but it reflected to God and to those around Mr. Taylor that he had made a decision to honor Christ and to lead his life in a way that demonstrated the seriousness of his decision.

Mr. Taylor was very devoted to his family, he cared deeply for his students and athletes, and he invested whatever time and energy that was needed to help them in any way. The joy in his life was obvious, and I wanted to have that joy in my life as well. After I prayed to receive Jesus as my Lord and Savior, Mr. Taylor quickly became an incredible mentor to me and helped me to understand just how I could let God work in my life as He did in his.

Whenever I would lose myself in the midst of competition and throw out profanity or be too hard on myself for not playing well, he would always be there to steer me back into control. Even though I was a new person in Christ, I still had many old tendencies that were extremely hard for me to change. I had a lot of anger issues deep inside that were hard for me to control, and sports became the avenue for me to vent those issues. Playing aggressively and using my anger as motivation had been my method of operation for many years. As I was beginning to learn how to use my walk with God as my sole empowerment on the field, I found myself in a constant struggle between trying to be a nice Christian boy and an aggressive, competitive athlete. As such, I wondered if being a Christian was in conflict with being the best athlete I could be.

Mr. Taylor was there for me the whole time. He laid the groundwork by example and instruction that I would later build on as my walk with God continued to grow. He helped me to understand that the Christian athlete is just as aggressive on the field as the non-Christian but never allows himself to lose composure.

Mr. Taylor's example, coupled with the support and example of my Christian peers, helped me to become a more stable person and a better athlete. Winning and having success were still the top priorities of my young life, but at least I finally had an idea of whom I wanted to become, and I had a support group of people who wanted to help get me there. As I grew as an athlete during my high school days, I grew just as much in my faith in Christ. My success in sports and my drive to achieve my dreams began to push me closer and closer to God. I was realizing more and more that He was the reason for my success and my talents, and that without Him, I was not guaranteed anything.

I was also trying to prepare myself for whatever He had for me. Football became very important to me, but I wanted to be prepared if He had another plan for my life that did not include football.

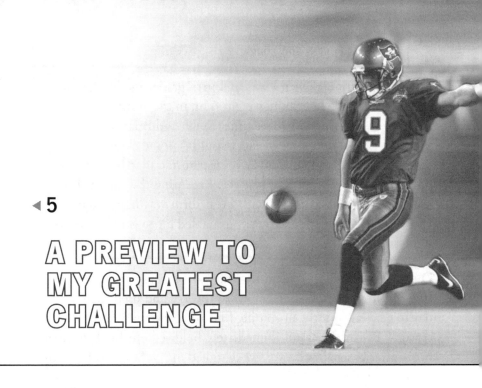

◀ 5

A PREVIEW TO MY GREATEST CHALLENGE

As I have mentioned before, sports consumed my life from the time I was old enough to walk, and in school I became quite serious about athletics. People began having high expectations for me as an athlete, and that only fueled the burning desire within me to work as hard as I could to make myself the best I could possibly be. Most of my friends were just as serious and driven as I was, especially Kevin and Brian.

Because Frank had been so passionate about strength workouts when he was younger, he set up a small weight-lifting room in a shed across the creek from their house. In this shed he had a squat rack, a weight bench for doing bench presses, and a small rubber mat to stand on when doing cleans. (A clean is a lift in which you squat down to grasp the barbell and then stand up straight and lift the bar to the front of your shoulders in one smooth motion.) Frank had a few dumbbells and weights, a small speed bag like boxers use, and other various exercise equipment. Kevin and Brian started lifting when they were pretty young.

I moved to Tenmile when I was in fourth grade, and by the time I was in sixth grade I began to weight train in the Tommasinis' shed. I was a very scrawny kid at the time. Kevin and Brian were already pretty muscular and strong, and I couldn't come close to keeping up with them. But Frank made it clear to me that I was not supposed to lift a lot of weight just yet. Executing the various lifting routines he designed for us with great form was more important. This early lesson in athletic training enabled me to get the most out of myself in all the sports I played.

During the summers, Kevin, Brian, and I set up various training stations around their large country property and used them every day to get ready for the upcoming football, basketball, and baseball seasons. Because football immediately followed our brief summer break after baseball was over, we designed most of our workouts to prepare for that.

The Tommasinis' property was unique. Their driveway led to a small parking area near the weight-lifting shed and a small concrete basketball court. This area was separated from the rest of their property by a small creek with a suspended footbridge. Crossing the bridge was a workout in itself! It swayed freely, and maintaining balance was tricky, especially with Kevin and Brian jumping up and down and rocking it as violently as they could whenever I tried to cross.

The main part of the Tommasinis' property comprised about ten acres of land, and we put it all to good use. We spent a lot of our free time creating new drills that improved our strength, speed, and coordination. Our training methods might have been a bit extreme at that young age, but the workouts were actually a lot of fun for us. We cleaned the underbrush from a small forest behind their house so we could make bicycle trails and forts.

The forest included a very steep hill that was about 60 yards long. We had seen an NFL video in which Walter Payton ran up a huge hill in the off-seasons to help strengthen his leg muscles and mental toughness. We decided to do the same thing and cleared all of the debris from the trail. Running just one full-speed sprint up that hill was exhausting, but we built up our endurance until we could run up to ten sprints. We designed many other speed, quickness, and jumping drills to maximize our athletic ability and mental toughness.

This may give the impression that I was wound a little tight as a kid, but nothing could be further from the truth. I made sure to have a lot of fun growing up. We loved playing wiffleball, but we always used a real bat so we could develop our swings. We discovered that a layer of duct tape over the outside of the ball enabled us to throw the most incredible curve balls. We could make the ball curve any direction we wanted, and that made it extremely difficult to hit. We knew that we would never see a real pitcher throw a real ball that would be as hard to hit as the pitches we were throwing to each other. So there we had it—a game that was an absolute blast to play that also helped us become better baseball players at the same time! (By the way, Brian and I still play wiffleball whenever we get home to hang out and visit with his parents. And we still use a real bat so we can maintain our swings…just in case a major-league team comes calling!)

By the time I entered Douglas High School, my work ethic was established, and my goals were well defined. I wanted to play on the varsity football, basketball, and baseball teams. My freshman year, I played two quarters of each game as the starting quarterback, free safety, kicker, and punter on the junior varsity football team, and then I played four quarters as the starting free safety, kicker, and punter for the varsity team. I was being groomed as the next varsity quarterback, and that was the position I most wanted to play. I had been a quarterback since I was in fourth grade and hoped to play that position in college.

I was fortunate to be at such a small school. Some of my college and pro teammates later told me that with so many kids in their giant schools, coaches had plenty of players to fill all of the positions on the field, and the players devoted their full attention to mastering one position. Some players said they even had to focus on just one sport, and their coaches discouraged them from playing anything other than their best sport. That was not the case for us. We didn't have a ton of players to choose from, so most of us had to play both offense and defense. We loved it! When I finally became the starting quarterback my junior year, I was on the field for every second of most of our games. I played offense, defense, and special teams, so I never had to come off the field except for time-outs and halftime.

As a freshman, I also started on the junior varsity basketball team and had a few opportunities to play on the varsity squad.

Douglas High School's baseball teams had been ranked number one in the state at some point in the season almost every year. They had an incredible amount of talent at every position, and forecasters were often sure Douglas would win the state baseball championship. However, as dominating as these teams were in their league every season, they always seemed to come up a game short in the play-offs.

My freshman year, I played for the junior varsity baseball team and was a reserve on the varsity team. I hit over .500 that season with a few home runs and played catcher. The varsity team rolled through their season as expected and were undefeated heading into the state play-offs. This season, however, we would not be denied. We reached the state championship game, where we won for the first time in the school's history. I was the only freshman on the squad and was there as an emergency reserve only, so I didn't get to play, but being there with the team was tremendous.

By the end of my freshman year, I'd had a great start to my high school athletic career. My hard work in training had paid off, and I kept up the momentum. As a junior, I finally became the varsity football team's starting quarterback and maintained my starting positions at safety, kicker, and punter. I was the first team all-league punter and kicker as a freshman and sophomore, and as a junior and senior I was also the first team all-league quarterback.

My junior year, our football team was the best our school had ever had. Kevin was the state's best linebacker and tailback. We topped our league, and in the state play-offs we reached the semifinals, only to lose that game in a downpour that created an absolute mud bowl. My first kickoff, which should have reached the end zone, was into such a strong wind that it only traveled about 35 yards in the air and was blown backward 5 yards.

Basketball was one of my favorite sports, but I was not what anyone would call a natural basketball player. In fact, our basketball team was very competitive, but our entire roster was made up of great athletes and not necessarily great basketball talents. Each season had its highlights though, and basketball offered us all a great venue to become better athletes and to physically prepare for the upcoming baseball season. My friends and I lived from sport to sport!

By my senior year, my walk with God was finally the most important aspect of my life. I knew, after studying God's Word, that He had a plan for my life, and I was eager to know what that was. I still had a strong ambition to play football in college and then professionally, but I also had a deep peace in my heart, assured that He had something great in store for me that might or might not include football. All I had to do was to work as hard as I could to achieve those goals, and if they did not happen, I would know that God had something else in His plan for me. That peace became even stronger the first time I thought my football days might be over.

I woke up early one morning midway through my senior football season, sweaty, dizzy, and in a daze. I lay there for a moment, taking inventory of my body, and I realized something was terribly wrong. I had been sick before; in fact, I seemed to get an extreme case of the flu at least once a year. But this was different. I had never felt this bad before, and my stomach hurt so much that I was unable to stand fully upright.

Very early in the morning, when my dad was in the living room getting ready to leave for work, I rose out of bed and managed to walk down the hall. Completely soaked from sweat and unable to see straight, I told my dad I wasn't feeling well and wouldn't be able to go to school that day. He said okay and watched as I walked back down the hallway to my bedroom, still hunched over and leaning hard against the wall to help keep myself from falling down.

By now, my dad could tell I was suffering from something more than just the flu. I lay down in my bed as he came in and asked me where I hurt and for how long. He then got on the phone and called the hospital. After describing my symptoms to the nurse, he decided to take me in right away so doctors could run some tests to determine what was wrong.

When we arrived at the hospital, the doctors quickly determined what was happening. They were sure I had appendicitis, and they gave me two options. I could either wait it out and see if the swelling of my appendix went down or I could have surgery to remove the appendix. They told me that if I decided to wait it out and the swelling went away, I would likely have the same problem again, and then I would be in danger of the appendix rupturing. Clearly, the wise choice was to have them remove the appendix to prevent any chance of this becoming a problem for me in the future.

After surgery, I woke up in my room and heard the doctor talking with my dad and stepmom. My appendix had actually ruptured sometime in the middle of the night while I was asleep. The doctor was extremely happy that we decided to heed his advice and go ahead with the surgery. Poisons had begun to spread from the rupture, but because I had the surgery, the doctors were able to get me on antibiotics right away to battle the infection and protect me from the danger of gangrene.

The timing of all this was such a blessing. That morning, had my dad and stepmom gone to work and left me home, I could have been in serious trouble. We lived about 30 minutes from the hospital, and I would have been stuck out there without a car. As I reflect back on that, I am grateful that God took care of that entire situation and that I ended up being just fine.

But what about my football career? This all happened with three games left in my senior season. I was in my second year as the starting quarterback. I was having a great season at QB as well as in kicking and punting, and the team had only lost one game. I was very optimistic that my senior season would win me a college scholarship. Now my season was over. I had performed well up to that point, but I wondered if it was enough. Very few people from our tiny high school had gone on to play major college sports. I was worried that missing those last three games would close any opportunities I had at a scholarship.

Fortunately, Mr. Taylor had been working hard to get videos of my highlights out to colleges for the past year and a half. I didn't realize the University of Oregon was seriously considering giving me a scholarship to compete for their punting and kicking jobs.

But amazingly, I wasn't sure if I wanted to go to college just to kick. I had been one of the star athletes my entire life. I wanted to be the next Dan Marino. I thought kickers were always the dorky guys on the field whose jerseys never got dirty. They were always the least athletic players on the field, and I didn't want to be saddled with being "just a kicker." Kicking had always come easy to me, and I did it because I was good at it and it was fun, but it was not my passion. I didn't know who all the NFL kickers and punters were. I didn't watch film on kickers or study the form of punters. I loved doing it, but thinking of moving on and being just a kicker was hard for me.

With all that I was contemplating, I made the wise choice of talking with Mr. Taylor about these issues, and he gave me some of the best advice I had ever heard.

"Josh, you only have one scholarship offer from a Division 1 school. The University of Oregon wants to give you a free college education and have you compete for a starting position on the football team. Are you seriously thinking about not taking it because you think kicking is not as cool as playing quarterback? You'd be a fool not to accept this amazing opportunity."

What great advice! I thought about what he said, and I talked with the Oregon coaches, who told me that if I wanted to I could try out for another position as well. I accepted the scholarship and signed my letter of intent to attend the University of Oregon on a full scholarship. I knew God had a plan for my life, and after the ruptured appendix, I was not too sure if it still included football. Once again, in His love and grace, He gave me a chance to fulfill my dream of playing college football and to get one step closer to my ultimate goal of an NFL career. My ambition of playing football in college had come true, and the next chapter in my life was about to begin.

Knowing that made the rest of my senior season so much more fun for me. I finished my high school career as one of the better athletes to have gone through Douglas High School, although certainly not the best. I finished my final basketball season as the team's highest scorer and rebounder, and I finished my senior season of baseball as the first team all-state catcher. I went on to win the MVP award in the state class 3A high school baseball all-star game.

My success in baseball made me waver a bit on my decision to go to Oregon to be a kicker and punter. After graduation, I played on a summer all-star team, and I led the team in home runs and finished near the top in batting average. I wondered if I had any future as a baseball player. But I had the chance to play with and against a few players who I knew were much better players than I was and who still were not high picks in the major-league draft. That confirmed my decision to accept a scholarship to play football. I was more passionate about football than I was about baseball anyway, so I was very peaceful about my final decision. I was excited to have played so well in my final year of competitive baseball, but my athletic life would never again be split between three sports. I was going to focus on football, and I couldn't wait for the challenges that playing at the next level would bring.

6

COLLEGE—A FRESH START

Heading off to college was both exciting and scary. Coming from a small, poorly funded high school with meager facilities and equipment, I knew that the facilities at the University of Oregon would represent a major upgrade. On a recruiting trip, I had taken a tour of the university's athletic facilities, including their fairly new sports complex—the Len Casanova Center, named for a successful former coach and athletic director—which housed all the university's athletic offices as well as the football team's locker room, the weight room, and the medical facility. Also in the Casanova Center is a large cafeteria, where we ate as a team during the season, and a trophy area that houses the trophies from all the sports as well as the university's hall of fame.

Taking a tour of the facilities was pretty exciting as a high school kid who was hoping to get a chance to go there, but walking through the facility after I arrived as an actual member of the football team brought a completely different sensation. I remember thinking to myself that with these facilities at my disposal for the next four or five years, I could make huge gains physically to improve myself as a player. The weight room was ten times the size of what we had at Douglas High School and contained much more equipment. Oregon also had an amazing strength and conditioning coach named Jim Radcliff, who designed specific workouts to make each of us better athletes in every way. We did the best we could to work out hard in high school, but we didn't know a whole lot about the best way to train ourselves. I was very excited about having coach Radcliffe to design workouts for us.

The Douglas High School athletic facilities couldn't compare to what I saw at the University of Oregon. When I first signed my letter of intent, I felt as if I had really hit the big time, but that feeling was nothing compared to the way I felt walking around those great surroundings and knowing I was now a part of it all. That feeling made me very antsy to get started with practice and to see up close what major college football was all about.

Our football training camp began more than a month before school started. The players moved into the dorms as a team and had a chance to get to know each other as training camp began. Training camp was much harder than I had anticipated it being. I immediately noticed how highly skilled *all* of the players were. We all had been the best players in high school, and now we were about as good or not quite as good as those around us. It was a very sobering experience, and I would find out later in my career that the coaches spend a lot of time and effort talking with these young players each year and helping them through this very difficult transition. A lot of these guys were so good in high school that they never had to challenge themselves, so they were not mentally prepared to be second-best at their positions. A few of the guys struggled so badly that they nearly gave up and quit the team. But most learned how to handle this difficulty and went on to be successful football players. Seeing just how good everyone was was definitely a shock for me. However, I felt that I had the right work ethic and a bit of a chip on my shoulder to prove that I could play at that level even though I was from such a small town.

I arrived at training camp at the beginning of August. For almost a month our schedule never changed. We got up early in the morning and ate breakfast as a team. After breakfast, we headed over to the football facility and prepared for the morning practice. After the two and a half hour practice, we hit the showers and headed back to the dorms for a quick lunch before attending meetings to watch the video of that morning's practice. When the meetings were finished, we had about 30 minutes or so to get back to our room and take a quick power nap before we went back to the facility to dress for the afternoon practice, which was also about two and a half hours long. Immediately following the second practice, we went back to the dorms for dinner and night meetings to watch the film from the afternoon practice. When those meetings were finally done, we were off to our rooms to open up the playbook and learn the plays we needed to know for the next day.

The college practices were much more demanding physically than what I was accustomed to, and the mental grind made them twice as tiring. Our practices were extremely intense from start to finish with no down time at all. Each practice was divided into five- to fifteen-minute periods. When one period ended, the other immediately began, and we were required to sprint to the location of our next set of drills so we didn't waste any time. That pace was similar to what we did in high school, but the major difference was the intensity of every single drill. In high school, we all were playing more than one position and had to practice them all in one practice, so we had to pace ourselves a little bit so we didn't wear ourselves out. In college we never paced ourselves. We had assignments for the entire practice and were expected to compete in every drill. In addition, we ended each practice by doing different conditioning drills as a team, and these were pretty exhausting after all the hard work we had already done. All of a sudden, all those drills and workouts Kevin and Brian and I had done as kids did not seem so outrageous. The work ethic and stamina I had built over the years made my transition to the rigorous practices much easier for me to deal with.

During training camp, I worked very hard on my punting and was expected to be the punter for the season. However, my punting form was very raw, and the coaches worked hard to change some aspects of my form to make me more consistent and powerful. I did everything they asked, but the results weren't exactly what they were expecting. The advice I was getting was very good, but I was not picking it up as quickly as they wanted me to. The coaches soon realized that Matt Belden, the other freshman punter and kicker they brought in that year, was a bit more reliable as a punter at that point. He ended up winning both the kicking and punting duties as a true freshman that year, and I was given a redshirt year to try to get better and more consistent for the next season.

Redshirting simply means that I would not play in any games that year, but I would get an extra year of eligibility, so I could play four more years after that. College players get only four years of eligibility, and redshirting is a great way to let a kid mature a bit so he is better able to compete at that level. I was pretty disappointed not to have punted well enough to win the job, but I was excited to have an entire year to improve and to compete again in the next season.

True to their word, the coaches allowed me to try out for another position as well as compete for the punting duties that year. Because I was a pretty good athlete in high school, the coaches tried me at tight end. My body type fit the mold closely, and I could catch the ball well. They even tried me at fullback. However, they soon realized I was completely useless as a blocker. Finally, I ended up at wide receiver, and there I would spend most of my days on the scout team my freshman year.

That year on the scout team with all the other freshmen was a blast! Even though we never played in a game that year, we all had a great time. Practices were fun; we ran plays against the starting defensive unit to prepare them for that week's opponent, and our goal was always to beat the defense on every play. (We succeeded only a handful of times.) Having an entire year to grow and mature as a football player made all the difference for me. I came back the next year punting a little bit better and doing pretty well at wide receiver as well.

The University of Oregon football program had been average at best for many years. The teams of the past were usually not great teams. Seasons here and there were successful, but in those days, that simply meant having a winning record and perhaps going to a bowl game. The Ducks usually finished in the middle of the conference standings, never finishing last and never finishing first. In my first year at Oregon, the 1994–95 season, that would all change.

The preseason hype from all of the sports analysts was most definitely *not* directed at the Ducks. I don't recall where we were projected to finish in the Pac-10 conference that year, but it wasn't very high. We were not a powerhouse in the Pac-10, not a perennial challenger for the conference title. As the season began, we had no reason to think the Duck football program would fare any better than in years past.

Our first game was a home game against Portland State, a much smaller Division 1-AAA school. Oregon is a Division I-A school. This was David against Goliath, but this time Goliath won the battle 58–16. It was a great start to a promising season, but hardly a worthy test to gauge just how good the team might be.

The next two opponents were good tests though, and the results did not look good for the Ducks. We lost 16–36 on the road at Hawaii and suffered an embarrassing 16–34 home loss to Utah. I have to admit that I did not have a lot of expectations for the team after those games. I certainly couldn't have predicted what was to follow these two losses.

Our next game, which was our last nonconference game, was against the Iowa Hawkeyes. They were a good team that year, finishing 7 and 4 in the Big Ten conference and beating the Washington Huskies 38–18 in the Sun Bowl. They played us in Eugene, where we put together an amazing game and beat them 40–18. That was definitely a confidence builder for us. We needed that win for many reasons, but the biggest reason was that we needed to know we could win big games against big opponents.

For us that season, no opponent was bigger than the USC Trojans, our opponent the next week in L.A. At the beginning of the week, we found out that our starting quarterback, Danny O'Neil, had to go to the hospital because of a staph infection in his throwing hand. He was definitely out, and our capable but inexperienced backup, Tony Graziani, was tagged to make his first start against a great USC team. Surely this game was not going to end up well for the Ducks…or so everyone thought. We flew down to USC, where Tony had a phenomenal day and led the Ducks to a 22–7 victory over the Trojans, giving us two straight wins against teams most people thought we would lose to.

We were rolling, and nothing was about to stop us…well, almost nothing. Our next game was in Pullman, Washington, against the Washington State Cougars. They were an above-average team that year, and playing in Pullman is always a hard test for any visiting team. With a lot of hype and maybe a bit of overconfidence, we lost 7–21 in a game that we all thought we had in the bag. It was a huge disappointment, and even worse, it left us all confused and wondering just how good we were. Did we win our past couple of games as a fluke, or were we a good team that could bounce back from this disappointing loss and make this season a successful one? The answer to that question came in a very unexpected way.

For the next five weeks, we won every game, in every fashion, from routing Stanford 55–21 to barely beating Arizona 10–9. Some of our amazing plays will forever be a part of Oregon football history, and the most memorable by far was in our game against the mighty Washington Huskies. The Huskies had a habit of beating Oregon every season, usually by a huge margin. We had enjoyed a great season so far, but that did not guarantee that history would change.

The game was great from start to finish. We played very well and were ahead late in the fourth quarter, but with the game winding down, the Husky offense was moving the ball down the field, seemingly at will. With Washington on the Oregon 9-yard line, poised to score the game-winning touchdown, quarterback Damon Huard dropped back…he threw the ball to his left to a receiver near the end zone…and then it happened—freshman cornerback Kenny Wheaton stepped in front of the receiver, intercepting the pass and running it back 97 yards for the game-sealing touchdown, giving Oregon one of the biggest wins in school history. It was one of the most memorable plays I ever had a chance to witness in my college career. To this day, that play is known simply as The Pick and is considered to be one of *the* plays that set Oregon football on the path to a new level of success.

Our last game was against our intrastate rival, the Oregon State Beavers, at their stadium in Corvallis. We had a lot on the line—we needed to win that game to secure the conference championship and guarantee a trip to the Rose Bowl, and it went down to the wire. We finally beat them on a late fourth-quarter score to win the game 17–13. Oregon would be making its first trip to the Rose Bowl in 37 years.

The entire Rose Bowl experience was a lot of fun. During the week leading to the bowl game, both teams were in L.A. for a variety of events and for team practices at our designated practice facilities. Our team attended a couple dinners, a private tour of Universal Studios, and a behind-the-scenes tour of the floats for the Rose parade. We also had some time off for ourselves so we could see a few sights on our own or with our families.

When game day arrived, we were all extremely excited. We had to play the number two team in the nation, the undefeated Penn State Nittany Lions. They were the heavy favorites to win this game, and no one thought we had a chance. The first play of the game seemed to confirm that everyone was right. Ki-Jana Carter, Penn State's superstar running back, took the first handoff of the game and ran 83 yards for a touchdown. After the extra point, the game was barely a minute old, and we were already down seven points. Needless to say, we had a fight on our hands. We were able to tie the game at 14–14, thanks to Danny O'Neil's second touchdown pass of the game. Despite Danny throwing for a Rose Bowl record of 456 yards and leading the Ducks to more than 500 yards of total offense, Penn State ended our season of dreams, beating us by a final score of 38–20. But the success of our season set a new standard for Oregon's football program, and the teams to follow would be held accountable to reach and exceed the success that the 1994–95 team had achieved. What a way to start my college career!

That summer I worked hard in the weight room and on my punting, but as my second season began, Matt was once again declared the starting punter and kicker for our opening game at the University of Utah. My wide-receiver coach took me aside that week and told me I was going to make the trip as the last wide receiver on the list, but I was not likely to get any playing time at receiver barring an injury to the guys above me. Also, I was going to make the trip as the backup to Matt should anything happen to him. Kickers rarely get hurt in a game, so I went on that trip not expecting to play at all and simply looking forward to my first college road game.

I can remember running out of the tunnel and into Utah's stadium to the boos of the sold-out crowd and thinking the experience was one of the coolest I had ever enjoyed. The game got underway with us receiving the kickoff and our offense taking the ball all the way down the field and scoring on our first possession of the game. On the ensuing kickoff, it happened. I was not sure what to think as I watched Matt kick the ball as hard as he could off the tee and then limp off the field, holding his kicking leg in pain. Our trainers met him on the sideline. Matt had torn his hip flexor muscle and was unable to kick for the rest of the game. That is when I got the news from head coach Mike Bellotti.

"Well, Josh, are you ready? Matt's not going to be able to kick for the rest of the game so it's up to you."

I looked at him and said, "Yeah, Coach, I'm ready to go." I have to admit, I sounded more confident than I really was. I was extremely excited and extremely nervous at the same time. As the game continued on, all of the kicking duties were up to me.

My first opportunity came when our offense stalled on fourth down and we were forced to punt. I went in there, caught the snap, and punted a mediocre punt down the field—nothing too bad, but not that great either. On our next possession, our offense drove down the field until they were finally held on fourth down on Utah's 25-yard line. That's when I heard Coach Bellotti call out for the field goal unit.

Oh my goodness! I thought. I ran up to him and said, "Are you sure?"

He looked at me a bit perplexed and said, "Yes—field goal! Get out there and kick it!"

I turned away as I ran on the field and lined up for a 42-yard field goal. To say I was nervous is an understatement. The snap came back, the holder put it down, and I approached the ball and kicked it. I looked up as the ball barely rotated and went straight up in the air. It seemed to be in the air forever before finally coming down, barely clearing the crossbar for three points.

I had done it! I had made my first college field goal! I went on to miss another field goal attempt but later made an extra point. We ended up winning the game by seven points, and I felt great knowing that my 42-yard field goal helped make the difference.

After the game, I approached Coach Bellotti in the locker room and said, "How about that, Coach? My first field goal!"

"Yeah, congratulations," he replied. "Your first college field goal. You deserve it—you've worked really hard for this."

I said to him, "No, Coach, that was my first *ever* field goal. I never made one in high school!"

He looked at me with a huge smile and said, "Wow, it's a good thing I didn't know that at the time. We might have gone for it!"

When we got back home, Coach called me in and told me I would not be allowed to play other positions anymore. We didn't have any other kickers to back me up, and he didn't want to put me at the risk of injury during practice by allowing me to run routes at wide receiver. This made perfect sense to me, but it was still a hard transition to make.

The rest of the season I was the starting punter, and we were able to bring in another kid to kick field goals, which was something I wasn't great at. My talent was punting, so that is where I would stay.

Unfortunately, Matt was never able to fully recover from that terrible injury he suffered in the Utah game. After trying to recover for the next couple years, he realized his injury was so severe and in such a vulnerable area that kicking would put too much stress on that injured muscle, never allowing it to fully heal again. This was such an unfortunate way for me to begin my career. Matt was a good friend of mine, and I was heartbroken to see my career begin only because his ended. I knew God was doing far more in my life than football, and by no means did He cause an injury to Matt so I could move in and take over. He knew what was going to happen, and He used all that I had learned so far in college and would use this situation to develop His plan for my life.

The rest of that season was a bit of a struggle at times. I only averaged about 36 yards per punt, which was one of the lowest averages in the Pac-10 conference that year. A decent average is about 40 yards per punt, and an elite few of the nation's punters average 45 yards per punt. I still couldn't fix some problems in my form and that kept me from kicking a great ball most of the time. When the season ended, I was excited to be the starting punter for the team, but I also knew I was going to have to work hard and improve to keep my starting job for the next three seasons.

The school year came to an end, and all the players were free to spend the summer any way they wished. Some players went home, and others decided to stay in town, either taking classes or getting a summer job. I had already decided to stay in town for the summer so I could work out with my strength and conditioning coach and work hard on my punting.

Just as school came to an end, I got a call from my Grandpa Stan, who had a big surprise for me. He told me that his business partner and best friend in San Diego knew Darren Bennett, the all-pro punter for the San Diego Chargers. Grandpa told me he had set up a weeklong trip and wanted to fly me down to San Diego with him and Grandma to meet with Darren and work out for a week with him. I could hardly believe what I was hearing! My grandpa was so proud of me for what I had done in school and in sports, and he knew that this trip was something I would never expect and that it would be a great experience for me.

Darren Bennett was one of the best punters in the NFL at the time. I was extremely excited to be able to pick his brain a little bit and watch him punt to see what I could learn that would help me to improve my own punting for the next season. We agreed that I would meet Darren on Monday, Wednesday, and Friday to go to the Chargers' practice facility to punt for an hour or so.

I was blown away by Darren's graciousness. He drove out of his way to pick me up where we were staying and drive us to the practice facility for the workout. From the first day we met, he was as nice as any person I had ever known. I didn't really know what to expect, but I didn't anticipate that he was going to be as friendly as he was. I was surprised by his humility. Had I not known his reputation, I would never have guessed it from the normal, plain-looking car he drove and the way he made me feel comfortable around him.

The first day, Darren took me to the Chargers' facility and gave me a tour of the locker room. I remember walking around in awe as I looked at the lockers of all the players and saw the Chargers logo painted everywhere. My dream was to make it to that level, so to walk around an actual NFL facility was great. I knew that not everyone gets a chance to do that, and the time went too fast. Darren and I then headed out to the practice field to punt together. The first time I saw one of his towering punts, I was pretty much ready to pack up my bags, go home, and quit. He had one of the strongest legs I had ever seen. I thought the missiles he was launching would never come down.

A punt is measured in a couple of different ways. The punter stands 15 yards behind the long snapper, so when a ball is punted, the length of that punt is actually measured from the place where it was snapped from—the line of scrimmage—rather than from where the punter actually kicked the ball. So if a ball is punted 45 yards and was actually kicked from about 11 yards behind the line of scrimmage, the ball literally traveled 56 yards in the air. However, the official stats record it as a 45-yard punt.

Three main stats are recorded for each punt. The first two are the gross punt distance and the net punt distance. The gross punt distance is what I just described, and the net punt distance is where the ball is stopped at the end of the play. For example, if a punt returner receives a 50-yard punt and runs it back for 10 yards, the gross punt distance is 50 yards, and the net punt distance is 40 yards. The third stat is the hang time. That is simply a measurement of how long the ball was in the air. The ideal is a 40-yard punt with 4.5 seconds of hang time. Punters want to be close to or higher than those numbers on each punt. After my low 36-yard punting average my redshirt freshman year, I had a lot of work to do.

The best punts spiral and turn over in the air. When a quarterback throws a ball, it spins fast, and the front of the ball starts facing up, gradually levels out, and then falls downward at the end of its flight. This allows the ball to aerodynamically cut through the air, enabling it to travel higher and farther. Punters try to make the ball do the same thing, and this was what I struggled with the most. I had as strong a kicking leg as any of my peers, but I could not figure out how to kick a great spiral consistently. That was the most important improvement I needed to make if I ever wanted to be a great punter and have a chance at punting in the NFL. I hoped that by punting with Darren, I could learn something from him that would help me to be much more consistent and would enable me to take full advantage of my strong leg.

As we worked out that day, he told me from the beginning that there was not too much he could tell me but that I would learn by watching him punt and asking questions. I noticed from the start that he was holding the ball differently than I did and dropping it a bit differently as well. I tried a few new things as he watched, and he gave me a few insights into what he was seeing as I kicked as well. I improved a few things on that first day with him, but I was still a bit intimidated by his ability. I knew I wanted to get to the NFL, but after seeing him fire those rockets, I was not too sure I was ever going to be strong enough to get there myself. He was consistently punting the ball more than 70 yards in the air (from where he was actually kicking the ball), and he had some punts that were in the air for as long as 5.5 seconds. Those were numbers I had not yet hit even once, but he was doing it over and over. Just having a strong leg is not good enough. Great punters consistently kick a great ball. That was where I was falling short. I was not consistent at all. I had been having a very difficult time kicking a great spiral and reaching those ideal length and hang time numbers, and I was hoping that by watching Darren I would be able to gain some insight that would enable me to become much more consistent than I had been.

On Wednesday, I waited for Darren to pick me up for another workout, but he wasn't there at the time we had set. I waited a little longer and then headed down the driveway and back to the house. On my way back, I heard my grandma call from the house that Darren was on the phone. I picked up the phone and heard Darren on the other line.

"G'day there, mate," he said. "I'm very sorry for not being there today and for not calling you earlier. My wife went into labor early this morning, and we just had a baby boy."

I guess that was a good enough excuse for standing me up! "That's great!" I said. "Congratulations! Please don't feel as though we have to meet again. I completely understand that you have your wife and son to concentrate on."

"Oh no, mate," he replied. "I'm hoping you can meet me tomorrow instead, and we can still work out on Friday too if you want."

I was blown away. I had never met someone who was so respectful of others. In the middle of one of his life's most amazing experiences, he was gracious enough to call me to tell me he couldn't make our appointment that day. I wouldn't have thought less of him if he hadn't called until the next day.

Darren told me that between contractions, when his wife was sure the baby was coming soon, she made him leave the room to call me because she was worried about me not knowing that he was not going to be at our workout. To this day, that example of respectfulness to others is something I try hard to emulate.

The next two days, Darren showed up on time and took me to the field. He was an incredible person to spend time with, and I picked up a lot of pointers from him that I was excited about working on for the rest of the summer.

I returned from my trip as motivated as ever. I worked very hard, and every week I improved. The most important change to my punting was my consistency. I was soon able to hit a strong spiral almost every time and was consistently exceeding 40 yards and 4.5 seconds. At every workout, I set up a couple of markers that represented a 50-yard punt, and I tried to kick beyond those markers every time. This ended up being a great drill that helped me to improve.

As I entered my sophomore season, I was a completely different player. The difference between my first season and every other season was like night and day. My gross punting average went from

36 yards as a redshirt freshman to 41.5 yards as a sophomore, and I continued to improve my stats each of the next two seasons. In my junior season I averaged 42.5 yards, and I had a true breakout season in 1998 as a fifth-year senior, averaging 46 yards per punt, shattering the school's single-season record (previously held at 43.7 yards per punt) and finishing second in the nation in gross average. I also led the nation with a 41.8-yard net average and was a second-team all-America selection by the Associated Press and *Football News* magazine. I additionally earned first-team all-Pacific-10 conference recognition for the first time and won the Gordon Wilson Award as the Ducks' special teams player of the year. I had one lone blocked punt in my collegiate career—in my senior year against Stanford—which snapped a string of 189 consecutive punts without a block.

I can look back and see that the week I spent with Darren made a huge difference in my college career, and I will always have the utmost respect and gratitude for Darren, for his wife, and for the favor they performed for a young man they had never met.

7

A NEW PERSON IN A NEW PLACE

ootball was not the only thing on my mind when I went to college. Since I had become a Christian my sophomore year in high school, I had been struggling hard to build up my new life with God. I was excited to be on my own and have a fresh start in a new environment, but I was pretty scared about being a Christian in college without all the spiritual support I enjoyed back home. This would be my first time on my own as a Christian, and life as a college student was sure to bring its challenges and temptations. I was determined to establish myself as a strong Christian right away because I knew that if I didn't, I would struggle later. I also wanted God to know I was serious about my new life with Him, and I wanted to use my time in college to do what He had planned for me to do.

I visited the local Christian store and bought about eight Scripture T-shirts, which I wore almost every day. I was a bit shy about my faith because I did not know very much Scripture, so I figured if I was not going talk to people very much about my faith, they could at least read about it on my shirt.

I quickly became the butt of some jokes from my unbelieving team-mates, but they also respected me when they realized that my faith was real and that every area of my life reflected my commitment to God. Living in that environment as a Christian was hard at times because I didn't have to hang out with anyone and be accountable. After all, I was on my own and could do whatever I wanted when-ever I wanted. No parents were around checking in on every detail of my days and holding me accountable for my actions.

Fortunately, I did hear about a few mature Christians on the team. Our star quarterback, Danny O'Neil, was a strong Christian leader, as were a few other guys. But the team had more than 90 players, and the vast majority of them were not Christians. I connected well with the few believers I had the brief chance to sit down with during those busy first few weeks, but we weren't able to enjoy focused times of fellowship, nor did I get the chance to really connect with any of my Christian teammates in the way I would have liked. We just didn't have opportunities to get together for more than a few minutes at a time and talk about anything other than football.

My first month and a half in college was dedicated to football. No students were in school yet, so I didn't get a chance to meet any believers who weren't part of the team. However, the very first day of classes, God blessed me beyond measure.

Students from all over the country were moving into the dorms. It was a hectic day to say the least. All of us football players had to move out of the rooms we were assigned to for training camp and into the rooms the school had designated for us. After moving my stuff into my new room, I wandered the halls, meeting people who were setting up their rooms and moving stuff in. I enjoyed seeing new people who didn't have anything to do with football.

As I made my way down to the main lobby, I saw a sign that said, "Athletes in Action, Campus Crusade for Christ." Under the sign, two people sat at a table that had another sign taped to it that read, "Would you like to know God?"

Holy cow! You have to be kidding me! I had been nervous about where I would go to church, how I would meet other Christians, and how I would find someone who could help me in my walk and knowledge of God's Word. During my entire childhood, supportive people just seemed to show up. I had mentors and friends who knew the Lord and were always there to invest in my spiritual life. But when I went to college, none of them would be there with me. I knew I needed to make new relationships to fill those roles in my life. I never had to do that before, and I didn't have a clue as to how I would make that happen. But all of a sudden, God took care of it for me once again.

I walked up to the table, wearing my Scripture shirt, and introduced myself to the two men sitting there. Their names were Dusty Davis and Matt Leighton. Dusty was the campus Athletes in Action director, and Matt was on staff with AIA working for Dusty. Athletes in Action is a Christian organization that helps athletes develop their walk with Christ. They are affiliated with Campus Crusade for Christ, which reaches the general student population in the same capacity. Dusty and Matt handed me a small questionnaire to fill out. The questionnaire asked my name and phone number, and at the bottom were a few questions with check boxes next to them: Would you like help finding a local church? Would you like to be a part of a Bible study? Would you be willing to meet one-on-one with someone about your faith? I don't remember all of the questions, but I do remember checking yes in all of the boxes.

Later that night I received a call from Matt. He was excited to see my responses on the card, and we set up a lunch meeting for the next day. After we ended our call, I was amazed that God had taken care of the aspect of my new life on my own that I feared the most. I went to college shy and terrified about developing my spiritual life and meeting people to help me along the way, and on the very first day of school, God took care of it. His timing was perfect. I knew at that moment that God was going to make sure I was taken care of. That day He gave me some wonderful friends that would help me along the way.

Matt and I met for lunch the next day. He was about 25 years old and had been a college quarterback at Brown University before joining the Athletes in Action staff. He was only about five-nine at the most and 175 pounds soaking wet, but he was a great athlete and had a ton of energy. Most impressive to me, though, was his passion for Jesus. We talked about our lives growing up and how we came to give our lives to Christ. He was very interested to know where I was at in my relationship with Christ and what I would need most when we started studying together.

Matt and I quickly become great friends. We hung out all the time. He took me to Athletes in Action Bible studies, where many of the Christian athletes on campus convened at Danny O'Neil's apartment. Matt, Dusty, or Danny usually led those meetings. The messages were mainly designed to develop the athletes' knowledge of God's Word and teach us to use the platform of our sport to spread the good news about Jesus to others. But for me, it went way beyond that. Even though I had been a Christian for a couple of years already, I was still very insecure about who I was. Matt and Dusty taught me about who God said I was and the potential I had with Jesus as the Lord of my life. The truths I learned during the next years of college enabled me to speak the Word of God boldly to whomever would listen and to gain confidence in who God wanted me to be.

I immediately made myself available to Athletes in Action in whatever capacity Matt and Dusty needed me. The summer after my first year of college, I attended the Athletes in Action weeklong summer camp held in Fort Collins, Colorado. It was one of the most powerful weeks of my entire spiritual life. I learned more in one week and gained more confidence during that time than ever before. The premise of the entire camp was summed up in one verse: "Whatever you do, work at it with all your heart, as working for the Lord, not for men" (Colossians 3:23). We learned how to play more competitively than we ever had before, using our relationship with God as our sole motivation. We spent the week exploring what Jesus did for us in His life and on the cross. I had a better appreciation for my salvation, knowing that He died a painful death to save me from my sins and that by rising from the dead, He gave me the power to have a new life. I constantly remind myself of that in the midst of competition, and my performance is an expression of thanks to God for the opportunities He has given me. Playing for God doesn't make me less competitive; it actually makes me more motivated and competitive than before. This truth took me to a level of play I never could have achieved on my own.

My walk with God in college was not without its struggles though. I continued to struggle with anger. I was used to suppressing my anger off the field and venting it in my aggressive play in competition. However, as I grew in my walk with God, He began to teach me how to deal with my anger constructively.

For example, I enjoyed playing pickup basketball games in the campus rec center, and these were very competitive at times. With many different personalities on the court at one time and no referees, these games can be disasters in the making for a lot of competitive college guys. I was no different. I sometimes lost control and exploded with anger. However, I was in constant conflict. I knew I was supposed to be in control of myself at all times and represent my faith in Christ even in the most difficult situations, but by no means was that easy to do.

I usually started out well and let little things go. A player would make a bad call, commit a hard foul, or do a little trash talking here and there, and I wouldn't respond. But after a while, these irritations began to fester, and I would eventually lose it. Here I was, excited about a fresh start in a new environment and trying to walk with God in public and private, and I'd swear at some poor kid on the court in front of everyone. After this happened, I would immediately feel terrible. I'd ask myself why I allowed myself to do that. I knew what I was supposed to do, but I did the wrong thing anyway. What was going on?

I took a couple years to learn what God's Word teaches about resting in Him. He was trying to reveal to me that I did not have to hang on to my anger and channel it to the field or court of competition, but I could give Him all my attention, and He would help me release that anger. It was a hard lesson to learn. When I think of some of the things I said and did to others in my first couple years of college, I wish I could take them back. I thank God that He has allowed me to give Him all my anger and anxiety, and in return, He gives me peace, joy, and purpose as He guides me in His will for my life. I missed out on some great opportunities to be an effective witness to other students. But God is faithful, and I'm thankful He is teaching me to keep my emotions under control.

Midway through my second year, Matt told me God was calling him to move to Spain for a ministry opportunity. He knew how much I had grown to depend on him and that I was going to be pretty disappointed. When he told me he was moving, he said I would be meeting with Dusty, who was a great guy and who would help me out immensely in my spiritual development.

He was right. I was bummed that he was leaving because he had become one of my best friends, and I was going to miss him terribly. And although I had heard Dusty speak at a few Bible studies and had seen him at barbecues here and there, I had never really gotten to know him. Like most people, I don't go looking for change in my life when things are going well, and I felt that my spiritual growth under Matt's guidance was definitely progressing. Matt's leaving was going to shake that up, and I was going to have to meet with this "old" guy who had three kids. (He was actually only 29 or 30 at the time, but I was only 19, so that was old to me!)

When I first met with Dusty, I felt as if we had been friends for years. To this day, I have never met a more passionate, giving, and genuine individual. Other people have impressed me in much the same way, but none have exceeded Dusty's qualities. After getting together with Dusty, I felt silly that I had ever thought he was too old and our lives were too different for us to connect. I couldn't have been more wrong. If I had chosen not to give him a chance, I would have missed out on one of the most amazing friendships I have ever enjoyed.

One of the most important things I learned from Dusty came indirectly to me through his life. I took notice early on in our relationship that he was mindful of God in his life at all times. I was so impressed with the way he could see God in movies, in newspaper articles, or even in a football game. He often sat with me and pointed out how something he read in the paper reminded him of a spiritual truth or how blessed he was to see a Christian athlete represent his faith in Jesus while on the field. That was a new concept to me. I was so used to separating my life with God from any environment that required my full attention or that I felt did not apply to Him directly. I never abandoned my faith, but I was missing out on the blessing of seeing God work and speak to my heart in every situation. Dusty taught me a rich lesson about keeping my mind on God at all times and letting Him have more of a grip on my thoughts and perceptions of life's events.

Dusty told me that as he rode his bike through campus and past my apartment, he prayed for me. As he rode his bike over a local footbridge that crossed the Willamette River on his way to our football practice, he prayed for the people he had the privilege of baptizing on the banks of the river below. He always used an article of some sort in a study or after-practice prayer meeting that illustrated a great truth about God and made His presence in our lives even more clear to us. To Dusty, God was everywhere, every second of every day.

This powerful perspective of God in my life was exactly what I wanted. As I began to apply Dusty's example to my own life, I began to experience God in a new and deeper way. He was changing me into the new person that He had created me to be, and I was enjoying the peace of God that transcends all understanding, as Philippians 4:6 describes to us. Peace from God is unlike anything we can manufacture on our own power, and thanks to Dusty, I was experiencing that peace in my life too.

But could I sense God's peace even on the field? I had grown up thinking I had to be angry during competition. I learned how to channel that anger into aggression that I used to dominate my opponents during games. This was what I saw on television when I watched college or pro games, and so I just assumed that was the norm and applied it to my own life. After becoming a Christian, I felt as if I were caught between a rock and a hard place. How could I be a tender Christian while on the field? How was I supposed to act like Christ and be an aggressive athlete at the same time? This was a very hard issue for me to deal with. For a while, I actually thought that being a Christian meant that I was not supposed to be as aggressive as I used to be on the field so that others could see my faith as I played. Even after the Athletes in Action camp, this remained a real frustration for me, and at some point I decided I would just do what I had to do while on the field and then be the kind, Christian guy I was supposed to be off the field.

A few days after one of our home games, Dusty and I met for lunch as we often did, and as usual, he answered a lot of spiritual questions I had and led me through a few studies to help me grow in my knowledge and my faith in Christ. After chatting for a bit, Dusty got right to the point.

"Josh, I wanted to talk to you about something I noticed you did in this last game."

I suddenly felt as if I were sitting in the principal's office, but he continued in an extremely loving and caring way. I could tell he was genuinely concerned about me.

"Josh, I know that you're working very hard to become stronger and stronger in your faith. I also know how important it is to you to be a great witness and leader to those around you. I just want to make sure that everything is okay with you."

"Yeah," I said, "everything is great. Why are you asking?"

"Well, I want you to know that I'm only bringing this up because I know it will be important for you to hear and because I care about you as a brother in Christ. During this last game, I was sitting about twenty rows up from your bench when I heard you drop a huge F-bomb after a bad punt."

I felt like shrinking into my chair.

He went on. "I know how important your witness is to others. A lot of kids and fans in the stands heard the same thing I did."

He was right. I was disappointed in myself, and I was also embarrassed to know that so many people heard me lose control like that. Of course, swearing is not the unforgivable sin and won't ruin others' lives. And I'm not pretending that the worst thing I could ever do is to use improper language. But that was definitely not the best way for a follower of Jesus Christ to speak. Dusty reassured me that I was fine, but he reminded me that it was extremely important for all of us believers to keep tight reins on our tongues so we could effectively represent God in our lives.

It was one of the most loving reprimands I've ever had. I assured him that everything in my life was fine, but I also confided in him that I struggled a bit with some anger that was still stored inside of me. I also confessed that I still didn't know how to be a Christian on the field without having to be a wimp, and I was going to need some help maintaining my competitive edge while representing Christ. He told me that he realized this was not an easy issue to overcome.

Each summer, I went with Dusty and a few other Oregon athletes back to the AIA camp I had attended after my first year of college. We continued to learn biblical tools to help us to draw on Christ for our strength rather than to use hidden anger or hatred to fuel our aggressiveness in the heat of battle. The camp's main goal was to teach all of us Christian athletes how to be as aggressive as or even more aggressive than everyone else out there, but to glorify God rather than ourselves. We studied the Scriptures and learned to play our sport as hard as we possibly could, within the rules of the game, as a thank-you performance to God for the abilities and opportunities to compete He has given us. Rather than just speaking words of thanks to God for His greatness in our lives, we learned to pour our whole hearts out to Him on the field in our play, honoring Him for who He is and what He has given to us.

This is an easy truth to talk about but a hard one to apply at times. On some days, things just do not go well, and we tend to focus on those bad times rather than to use those moments to compete as hard as we can and offer that maximum effort as a thanks to God. If I am not careful, I will still fall short in this area and focus on appearances rather than God and His work in my life. Without Him, I would not be in the NFL, and I am privileged to try to dominate on every single play solely to glorify Him. This is a powerful truth that changed my life and made me an even better football player. It never changes, and I still try to apply it as I take the NFL field each Sunday.

And if I ever have to sit in the principal's office again, I hope the principal will be Dusty Davis.

8

THE GIRL OF MY DREAMS

I found more than just great teaching at the Athletes in Action meetings. I also met the girl who would become my wife.

After Danny graduated, my roommate and I hosted Dusty's AIA Bible study at our apartment on campus. One particular evening, I was sitting on the floor next to a good buddy, Ryan Schmid, as people were streaming in the front door. He and I had only been talking for a few minutes when a girl walked through the door and took my breath away! I will never forget that moment. She was the most beautiful woman I had ever seen. If I had ever put together in my mind what the perfect woman would look like, she fit every description perfectly, and the most important part was that she loved the Lord. I had to meet her.

As it turned out, Ryan happened to be one of her good friends, and he lived in the same dorm she did. I leaned over and asked him, "Who is that?"

He took one look and said, "Oh, that's Bethany Smith. She's a freshman on the softball team. Why do you ask?"

That question needed no response as I looked over at him and gave him a glimpse of the glow on my face. He could tell right away exactly why I had asked about her.

"Bad news though, buddy," Ryan said. "She's actually seeing someone right now."

I was so bummed. It was not my custom to try to move in on a girl who was in a relationship with someone else, and this situation was no different. For the rest of that school year, Bethany came to every study with a few of our common friends, and we got to know each other a bit hanging out in a big group on weekends. She didn't know at the time that I liked her, but that would change when I got the news that her other relationship had ended.

Ryan was on a mission to get the two of us together. He often arranged for us to be in the same place at the same time at movies, barbecues, and other campus events. He even made sure that when a group of us went to a movie, all the seats would be taken in the car and Bethany and I would be "forced" to ride together in mine.

I eventually worked up the nerve to call her on my own to ask if she wanted to hang out or to invite her to events with the group. She had no idea at the time that I liked her, and in fact, she didn't seem all that interested in a relationship. I eventually quit calling her and tried to move on.

She tells me that was actually a pretty good move on my part. When I stopped calling, she began missing hanging out with me, and she actually started trying to contact me from time to time. I was still so smitten with her, I wasn't sure I could handle just being friends. I was a bit hesitant to respond to her calls, not wanting to get my hopes up too high.

Bethany finally erased all of my uncertainty with a simple 30-second visit that caught me completely off guard. I was in my senior season at the time and a day away from taking my last college road trip. My roommate and I were sitting in our apartment on campus, talking about Bethany and me. I told him I was sure she didn't want a relationship with me and that I was going to stop hanging out with her because I couldn't look past my feelings for her and just be friends.

Not more than two minutes later, we heard a knock at the door. I opened the door, and Bethany stood right there staring at me with a small bouquet of flowers and a card. She was just stopping by to give me those gifts and to wish me well on the last road game of my college career. I told her thanks, and she left. I opened the card with my roommate right there and saw what she had written inside. She left no doubt that she had grown to like me as much as I liked her and that she was excited that God had brought the two of us together. I couldn't believe it! I had obviously been pretty clueless.

By the time my season ended, Bethany and I were spending a lot of time together. I was smitten from the start and my feelings for her grew every day we were together. On November 4, 1998, Bethany and I had a very straightforward talk and officially began dating. Bethany actually made fun of me a couple years later when I told her I remembered that date. She said I couldn't possibly remember the exact date we officially started dating. But soon after she challenged my memory, she received an e-mail from one of her best friends that included an old e-mail Bethany had sent her. She thought Bethany would want to have it as a keepsake. The date of the older e-mail was November 5, 1998. In it, Bethany told her friend about the great time she and I had the day before and that we had both revealed our feelings and were officially dating.

Even a clueless guy can have a good memory.

9

CROSSROADS TO THE NFL

My senior year had come to a close, and Bethany and I were at a crossroads in our relationship. We had been dating for only a few months, but we had fallen head over heels in love with one another. Our future was uncertain at the time—I was getting ready to try out for the NFL, and she had just quit playing softball to fulfill a lifelong dream of spending a few months working in a church in Costa Rica. Neither of us knew if our dreams would be fulfilled, but we were certain we would do all we could to make our relationship work.

Between the end of the college season and the April 18 NFL draft, I worked my tail off. I had set up about five workouts with NFL coaches who came to the University of Oregon campus to watch me kick. These sessions each lasted about an hour or so and consisted of me kicking in different parts of the field as they were directing. Each workout was an absolute thrill for me. Most of them went very well, but I had no idea if they were going well enough to get me a spot on an NFL team. The workouts stopped just before the NFL Scouting Combine.

The Combine is by invitation only. It is held in Indianapolis, Indiana, in the RCA Dome, where the Indianapolis Colts play. The NFL flew me and about 20 other kickers and punters to Indianapolis for all kinds of physicals, testing, and a kicking workout on the final day. The first couple of days were a whirlwind. We all had to go from room to room to get checked out by doctors of all sorts. They checked the strength of our knees and our legs. They hooked us up to all kinds of machines to assess our health. They looked at our hearts, our circulation, our breathing, and everything else you can imagine. We filed into a room in just our shorts and were weighed and measured in front of all the team personnel who were there. Then we had individual interviews that were taped and given to all of the teams so they could listen to our answers and assess what kind of people we seemed to be. We also took a few written tests that were designed to help the clubs understand just what type of personalities we had.

The New York Giants, in particular, conduct a test that everyone hates. It's long and repetitive and includes some extremely weird questions. Why do they need a test that's ten times longer than all the others? I still remember some of the questions: Do you like to hurt animals? Have you ever hurt an animal and enjoyed it? If you were to hurt an animal, would that make you feel good? If you accidentally hurt an animal, would you feel sorry? Even with all our complaining, I hear that the Giants still use that same test today.

After all the physical and mental evaluation was completed, we were off to the field for a kicking workout. Representatives from every single NFL club were watching on the sidelines and taking notes on everything. The situation was incredibly intimidating. To see head coaches and general managers of NFL teams giving us their undivided attention was sobering; we only had ten kicks each, and all of them counted. Fortunately, I had a very good workout. Not all of my punts were great, but they definitely separated me from many of the other punters. Still, even though I felt I had a great Combine, I had no way of knowing what would happen on draft day. Kickers and punters are rarely drafted, so I was preparing myself to handle not getting drafted and having to earn a roster spot on a club as a free agent.

I spent draft weekend back home in Winston so I could enjoy a relaxing and "distracting" day in the comforting confines of the country. Brian Tommasini and I were on our wiffleball field playing home run derby, and my dad and Frank and Marge Tommasini were inside watching ESPN when I got a call. I grabbed the phone and heard a coach on the other end.

"Josh, this is Coach Steve Ortmeier out here in Green Bay."

I had met Coach Ortmeier, the special teams coach for the Packers, a few weeks earlier at a private workout. He asked me, "What are you doing right now?"

"Well, Coach," I said, "I'm actually playing home run derby with my best friend."

"Just trying to keep yourself from getting too anxious I guess, huh?" he said. "Well, Josh, let me get to the point. How would you like to be a Green Bay Packer?"

"Yes sir!" I said. "That sounds great!"

"Good," he replied, "because we just drafted you!"

Oh my goodness! I didn't know what to say except thanks. I was completely overwhelmed. The conversation continued with him telling me he had high hopes for me and thought I had a lot of potential. I obviously could not thank him enough for the opportunity.

My NFL dream had begun when I was four years old, sitting on my Grandma Cleone's lap and watching an NFL game with her on television. She was maybe five feet tall and less than a hundred pounds, but she was a huge football fan and full of energy—especially when Minnesota was playing. I looked up at her and told her I wanted to be a football player when I grew up. She told me that was great but that I should get a college degree too because a football career would not last forever. She was definitely rooting for me to reach my goal, but she knew for anyone to make it to the NFL was a long shot. She wanted to keep me grounded so I could have every opportunity to succeed in life.

Grandma Cleone was one of the first people I called on draft day to tell her the news. She was thrilled for me because she knew as well as anyone how important this was for me and how long and hard I had worked to get to that point. The memory is very special for me because only a couple months later my dear Grandma Cleone, lying in a hospital bed, passed away from heart failure.

Grandma Cleone was a special person in my life, and I am so thankful she was alive to see me get drafted to the NFL. In my last moments with her in her hospital room, I gave her an NFL ball and told her I loved her, that I was proud of her, and that she was a big reason my dream had come true. She had tubes in her mouth and was unable to talk to me, but I could see the immense pride in her eyes as she gestured the same feelings back to me. She passed away the very next day. I feel so fortunate and grateful that God gave us those moments together, and I know we will see each other again someday.

From the beginning, my dad had done all he could to support my dream and to encourage me. He had always supported me and believed in me, so for him to be with me on draft day made that day perfect. We took a picture together when I got off the phone with the coaches to capture the moment I had worked my entire life to achieve. I will never forget that day, and I was so grateful that my dad had a chance to be there and be a part of it as it happened.

Just a few years ago, I found a couple photos from my childhood and put them together chronologically, from a snapshot from my first days as a fifth-grade quarterback on my first flag football team, to a picture of Dad and me after a college game at the University of Oregon, and finally to that moment right after being drafted. I gave them to him and told him that as a kid, I had no way of ever knowing just how far my dreams would take me. Now, as I look back at his love, support, and guidance, I am sure he knew full well just what I was capable of. Under the photos representing a few pieces of my journey, I wrote a note to my dad: "Thanks for being by my side at every step of this amazing journey. I could not have done any of it without you. I love you, Dad!"

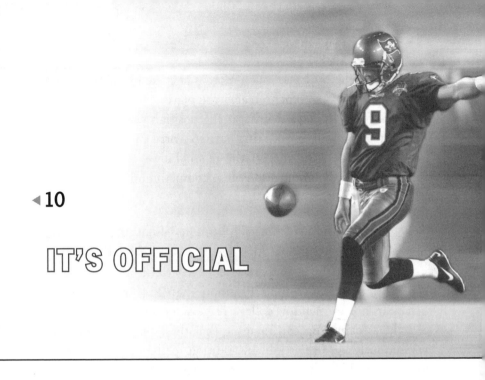

10

IT'S OFFICIAL

For the next couple months I remained in Eugene and continued to work out at the U of O football facility before heading off to Green Bay, Wisconsin, for training camp. I had already been to Green Bay for two three-day-long minicamps, so I had an idea of how practices would operate. The Packers' training camp is held at their normal facilities. Most teams in the NFL train at small colleges—almost exactly as the players did in college, but now their cars are a little nicer.

Even though our practices were at our facility, we all stayed in the dorms of the small St. Norbert College in De Pere, Wisconsin, just ten miles away. The schedule was just as busy as what I had experienced in college: an early wake-up call, breakfast, practice, lunch, meetings, a little time off, practice again, dinner, meetings, and bedtime.

The main difference between college camp and NFL camp is the intensity. Practices in college were definitely intense, but that was magnified in the NFL. So much more is at stake in the NFL, and the competition is so much greater, the players turn it up a notch to say the least. In college, my starting position was on the line if I wasn't playing well, but I didn't have to worry about the coaches firing me and kicking me off the team. However, in the NFL, players are always coming and going, competing for a position on the regular season 53-man roster.

At the start of training camp, each team has about 95 players, and that number fluctuates as guys get hired and fired throughout camp. But by opening day, every team has to be cut down to 53 men. With 32 teams in the NFL, more than 1340 players get cut each year, not to mention college players coming out and trying to make a team. You can imagine that these guys take football very seriously—it's their job. In addition to the players' competition, the coaches bring intensity to the field because their jobs are on the line as well. The teams' performance determines whether the coaches keep their jobs or are fired. I wasn't fully prepared for the intensity I experienced at the NFL level, but I soon realized that this was a business, and I was expected to perform at my best every day.

My favorite part of this new experience was my relationship with our field goal kicker, Ryan Longwell. Ryan and his wife, Sarah, both grew up in Bend, Oregon, only about two hours from where I lived, and Ryan played his college ball at the University of California in Berkeley. We didn't know each other in college even though we had played against each other a couple of times, but the fact that we were both from Oregon and both loved God dearly helped us quickly become great friends. Ryan and Sarah opened up their home to me when I first moved out to Green Bay about a week before training camp began. I really hadn't known them for very long at that point, but they treated me as though we had known each other for years. Our friendship from the start made my transition to the NFL so much easier and allowed me to enjoy the experience so much more fully. Ryan was always there to show me the ropes.

Starting training camp as a rookie right out of college was like starting a new school. Most of the guys on the team knew each other well, and a lot of them had been there for a while. It was also a bit strange to mingle with guys who were in their late twenties and early to mid thirties. A lot of these guys had children, some of whom were in middle school or even high school. Coming from a college team, where most of us were pretty close to the same age, I took a while to get used to this new environment. I was 23 years old and unmarried, so competing with and against more mature men was kind of weird. It was not a scary situation for me, just a strange one. We had a great lineman on the team named Frank Winters, who was in his sixteenth NFL season. I did the math, and that put me in fourth grade during his rookie season in the league. He got a kick out of that fact when I told him. I was definitely in a new world.

The first game of my NFL career was actually the first NFL game I had been to. It was a home game against the New York Jets. My first play was on a hold for a field goal attempt by Ryan. I had held for Ryan during training camp and was very comfortable doing so. Ryan and I ran onto the field together, and I couldn't help looking around at the stadium and drink in the moment. I must have gotten a little distracted. I knelt in preparation to receive the snap and put the ball down for Ryan to kick, and all of a sudden I heard Ryan calling out my name. He was laughing—I was on the wrong side of the ball. I was set up on the left as if he were a left-footed kicker when in fact he is right-footed. I was grinning ear to ear, Ryan was laughing his head off, and as we both looked down at our snapper, Rob Davis, we could see him laughing as well. No harm was done as I got up and switched over to the correct side, and Ryan kicked the ball through the uprights. This all took only a couple seconds, but it is something we still get a chuckle out of today.

My first two games were a bit of a struggle for me, and I was still competing against one other punter for the position at Green Bay. But as we headed down to New Orleans to play the Saints for the third of our four preseason games, it all began to come together. I had a great day punting and felt assured I was on my way to getting better and making a strong start to my career. We finished the game that Saturday and headed back to Green Bay that night.

The next day I got a call from my special-teams coach, Steve Ortmeier.

"Well, Josh, we cut the other punter. Congratulations—you're the starting punter for the Packers!"

It was official. My dream had come true.

After I hung up the phone that day, I couldn't help but pray a prayer of thanks to God for this amazing gift. All the hard work, all the advice and help from others (including that fateful ride home with my dad after our meeting with my sixth-grade teacher) had paid off. I called my family and close friends to tell them the great news. Many of those I talked to were under the assumption that I was already guaranteed the job, not realizing how much of a business it was. But I fully appreciated the magnitude of the situation and was overwhelmed that it had really happened.

After all the calls, I just sat and thought about being the starting punter for the Green Bay Packers. I was confident I was on my way to a long and successful career.

11

MY LIFE TURNED UPSIDE DOWN

We had Sunday off after the Saints game, but by Monday it was back to work again to prepare for our final preseason game at home against the Miami Dolphins. I was really looking forward to this game because the Dolphins were my favorite team when I was growing up, and their starting quarterback, Dan Marino, had been my favorite player. I had some Dolphins apparel and football cards, so I was pretty excited to play against the team I had watched so much when I was younger.

Monday night, while staying in a hotel with a number of my other teammates, I discovered a hard lump on my right testicle. I had no idea what it was. Something inside of me made me worry a bit about what this could be, but I tried to convince myself it was nothing and would go away in time. I was not tired, sore, fatigued, or anything else. I decided nothing was wrong and I would be just fine.

The next day it was on my mind, but I didn't bring it to anyone's attention. I just kept it to myself. But on Tuesday night, as I examined the lump again, I felt a pit in my stomach and sensed that something was wrong. I also remember hearing about a testicular cancer survivor who was a cyclist and had some sort of problem as well, but I did not know at that time that he was Lance Armstrong, nor did I have any idea of all that he had endured. But because I had heard something about him and his case, I resolved to take advantage of our free doctors and be rid of the anxiety I was feeling.

Wednesday morning, I went into the facility as normal, still wavering a bit as to whether I wanted to tell the doctor about it. I was feeling several emotions. I wondered if the doctor would hear about the area of my body I wanted him to look at, tell me I was just fine, and laugh it off. I was also a bit worried that I was overreacting and that this was something that was normal and that I hadn't noticed before. In either case, I would be a bit embarrassed by the whole situation.

When I finally went in, I found our head trainer, Pepper Burress, and told him of my situation. He told me he wanted to have our team physician look at it as soon as he arrived. About an hour later, our team physician, Dr. John Gray, showed up and called me into one of our examining rooms. As he examined the lump for himself, I remember feeling as though time stood still. I will never forget the look in his eyes after he felt the lump.

"Josh, this could be serious. I don't want to scare you, but lumps like this are sometimes cancerous, so we're going to have to set up an appointment with a urologist today to see what he thinks it might be."

I was shocked! I had been sure I was just fine and that he would tell me so. But when I saw his eyes and heard the urgency in his voice, I knew I was in a potentially dangerous situation.

The appointment was scheduled for 11:30 a.m., just a few hours later. In the meantime I was getting ready to head out to the field for the pregame walk-through we always have the day before a game. For half an hour or so, I just sat at my locker, worrying about what to expect when we went to the urologist. As Ryan and I walked down the tunnel leading out to Lambeau Field, I said to him, "Hey, buddy, can you pray for me? I just had an exam with Dr. Gray, and we're not really sure what's wrong, but I may have cancer."

He was a bit taken aback and looked into my eyes to see if I was kidding. When he realized I was serious and saw the fear in my eyes, he said he certainly would pray for me and that he wanted to know what was going to happen next. I told him I had an appointment set up already after practice to see exactly what was going on. Ryan couldn't believe it either. We went out to practice but had a hard time focusing on the task at hand. He kept coming over and asking questions and trying his best to assure me that I would probably be fine. We had no way of knowing whether that was true, but it helped the time go by a bit faster for me.

During the entire practice, I kept thinking to myself that I didn't feel any different. I thought people who had cancer were very sick and had all sorts of side effects. I had none of that. I wasn't sick, and I didn't feel anything at all, so I wondered if this was all a mistake and I had nothing to worry about. I was trying to convince myself that my visit to the doctor would confirm exactly that and all my worry was in vain. Little did I know that an hour later, my worst fear would be realized.

Immediately after practice, Pepper, Dr. Gray, and I went straight to the urologist to get an ultrasound and see what was going on. When we arrived at the office, we were immediately ushered to an exam room. Everything had been set up before our arrival, and the urologist was in the room waiting for us. After a quick introduction, the doctor got right to it and said he was going to perform an ultrasound to see what the lump looked like. I didn't know quite what to expect. I was not even sure what the ultrasound would look like or how conclusive it would be. The doctor turned the machine on, positioned the monitor so we could all see it, and used the controller connected to the ultrasound machine to take a look. He took all of about 15 seconds to see all he needed to see.

"Well, Josh," he said, "you have cancer."

He wasn't rude about it, but he was very matter-of-fact and came across as emotionless and a little cold. I couldn't help but grasp for a little hope that he could be wrong, so I asked him, "Are you sure?"

"Absolutely," he replied. "I'm sorry, Josh, but this is, without a doubt, cancer."

That was when the whirlwind began. The doctor told me I would need to have surgery that afternoon to remove the tumor so it could be tested to determine which cell type or types it contained. He said it could possibly be a seminoma, which he said was the "good cancer." Seminoma is nonaggressive and doesn't spread. He said it could be removed and that I could recover within two weeks and be able to play again. He thought this was probably the case, but he said we couldn't take anything for granted and would have to wait through the weekend for the test results to be sure.

By the end of the appointment, I had an outpatient surgery scheduled for a few hours later. We returned to the football facility so I could call my family and friends to tell them was what going on. No one back home had any idea what was happening. I didn't have time to call before the appointment, nor did I want to call home and cause people to worry before I had all the facts. But now I knew what was going on and the Packers were going to have to release the news to the media, so I wanted to make sure my family heard it from me rather than hearing about it on the news.

Pepper was particularly comforting to me and insisted that I use the privacy of his office to make my calls to my family and friends. I sat for a moment in his office, completely overwhelmed. I wanted to gather myself so I could keep my composure on the phone and not cause anyone to panic. It was still early, and all I knew was that I did have cancer but that it could end up being just fine if it turned out to be a seminoma. I was still pretty shaken, but I was holding out a little hope that I might be back playing in two weeks. That calmed me down a bit before I began to make my calls.

My first call was the hardest call to make. Now that I am a father, I can't imagine getting a call from my little boy and hearing that he has cancer. I called home, and my stepmom answered the phone. My dad was asleep at that time because he was working a night shift at the mill that night. I didn't really know what to say or how to say it, so I just asked my stepmom if she would mind getting my dad up and on the other phone. He got on the phone a little groggy. He wasn't prepared to hear what I was about to say, but I think he knew something was wrong. Not wanting to string them along, I got right to the point. I thought I calmed myself down before I made the call, so I was a bit surprised when my voice began to crack and tears started welling up as I began to talk.

"Well, I don't know quite how to tell you this," I said, "but this morning I came across a lump and had our team doctors look at it. They were pretty concerned about it and set up a urologist appointment for me right away, which I just returned from. He says I have testicular cancer."

I couldn't believe how hard that was to say, nor could I imagine how my dad felt, hearing that his son had cancer and knowing he was 2500 miles away. I could tell he didn't know what to say or think. He asked how I was, just as he had always been careful to make sure I am okay. I told him that I was all right, that the doctor said this could be seminoma, and that I might be fine. I told him

I had to have outpatient surgery that afternoon so the tumor could be tested over the weekend. By Monday, we would know what cell type or types comprised the tumor and what was next for me. My dad was obviously shaken.

My next calls were difficult as well. By this time it was pretty hard to keep my composure, knowing how concerned everyone would be at the news. I called my Grandpa Stan and Grandma Beverly next. They lived in Medford, where my mom and her side of the family lived. I knew that even though they would be floored by the news, they would be able to handle it and pass it on to the rest of the family for me. It was a difficult call; my relationship with my Grandpa Stan had always been strong. He had been so proud of me as I was growing up and made a lot of effort to be there for me in any way I needed him. I never heard my grandpa cry before, but I could almost see his tears as we talked. Still, I tried to assure him that I might be just fine in a couple weeks. He and my grandma offered to fly out to Wisconsin right away if I needed them to. I told them that would not be necessary because I had to wait to find out what might be next for me depending on the results of the biopsy.

I next called Bethany's family. Bethany and I had been dating for about nine months by then and knew that we loved each other dearly and wanted to be with each other when the time was right. Bethany had quit playing softball after her second year and was preparing to fulfill a lifelong dream of living in Costa Rica for a few months while working in a church. This was a dream that Bethany had worked hard to realize. She was studying (she has since graduated with a degree in Spanish from the University of Oregon) and was in Los Angeles for a week of training and preparation for the work she was going to do while in Costa Rica.

I was unable to reach her, and because my diagnosis was going to be in the news and I would not be able to speak to anyone until later that night after the surgery, I had to get a message to her right away. I called her parents' home so they could relay the news to her for me. Her younger brother, Nate, was the only one home at the time. I knew Nate well, but giving him the news and not being able to talk to Bethany's parents was a little weird. I wanted at least to give them the impression that there was a chance I would be okay. Nate was concerned for me and for Bethany. Bethany's family and I had gotten very close by then, and they would play a huge role in my recovery. Nate said he would get ahold of his parents and have them contact Bethany right away.

I made a few more calls and left for Ryan and Sarah's house for an hour or so before my surgery. They really took charge and made sure I was taken care of. They insisted that I stay with them after the surgery. The memory of the love and support they showed me back then blesses me still today. I felt as if they were family, and they took care of me as if I were.

Ryan and Sarah took me to the hospital for that first surgery to remove the tumor. The surgery took only a couple hours, and by the end of the day I was released to go home. Ryan and Sarah were there to pick me up and take me back to their house. The surgery was pretty minor, but I still had a hard time getting around without help. I was grateful for the two of them and needed more assistance than I had anticipated. They never seemed burdened and showed me time and again that they were only concerned about my well-being and recovery.

When I got back to the Longwells', several messages from Bethany were waiting for me. She wanted me to call her as soon as I could and said she was praying for me the entire day. I finally got a chance to call her late in the evening. I didn't realize how hard it was going to be to talk to her about what was going on, and being a bit weak from the surgery made it even harder for me to hold myself together. She had been waiting by the phone in her room in L.A. all day and picked it up on the first ring when I called.

She told me her mom, Laura, had called her and asked if she had talked to me yet that day. She said she hadn't and wanted to know why. Laura said Bethany needed to get ahold of me right away. That made Bethany panic a bit; she asked her mom what was going on. Laura told her what I had relayed through Nate, that I had been diagnosed with cancer and that I was going in for surgery that afternoon.

Bethany had been on an incredible high at the prospect of leaving the very next day for her dream trip to Costa Rica, but now her emotions plummeted. She asked if she should go out to Wisconsin to be with me. Laura knew Bethany would not be able to stop worrying about me, especially since she was scheduled to leave for Costa Rica. Laura and the family also knew that Bethany and I were deeply in love, and I think she knew very well that if she were in Bethany's shoes, she would want nothing else but to fly out and be with me. That's exactly what happened. Laura arranged for Bethany to fly out the next morning and postpone or possibly abandon her dream trip.

By the time I finally reached Bethany, her flight was already arranged. It was so good to hear her voice. Bethany and I were inseparable when we were back home together. The prospect of being apart for the season was heartrending, but for her to be in Costa Rica while I was in the middle of this trial would be much worse. I was excited to know that she would be with me that next day, but I was bummed that she was not going on her trip. I knew how much it meant to her and what she gave up to be able to go on it. At first I tried to convince her that I would probably be fine in a couple weeks and that she should go on her trip. She made it very clear that that was out of the question. Besides, she had already arranged her flight to Green Bay.

I loved Bethany from our first date. I could never have imagined the amount of love she would give me.

Brian Tommasini called me four or five times to see how I was doing. In each call, I could hear that he was very shaken up by the news. His last call that night revealed his struggle with what was going on.

"Josh," he said, "I've have been asking God all day why this had to happen to you. It's just not fair that you've gotten so far in life and so close to your dream, but now this happens to you. You don't deserve this. I don't understand what God is doing."

I will never forget that call. Brian was close to tears, and I could tell he had thought of nothing else that entire day. Hearing the pain in his voice and knowing he was close to tears almost made me lose it. But I made a decision from the first time I found out about the cancer that I would never ask God, *Why me?* I resolved deep inside to accept that God allowed this to happen to me for a reason. He trusted me enough to use this situation for His glory, and if I were to lose my life to this disease, I would go to my last breath sharing the reality of eternity and the truth that my faith in Jesus Christ would get me to heaven. To me the miracle is not surviving cancer but being saved from my sins and spending eternity in heaven with God because of my faith in Jesus Christ.

I told Brian exactly that. I was warmed by his concern, but I wanted him to know that God was not to blame. Rather, He had a plan for me that I was going to use as best I could. I told Brian I was scared but that I was also grateful that I had the opportunity to use this disease to glorify God. I know that was a big help for Brian as well as for me. To have that conversation with him reinforced my conviction to be as strong as I could.

I did not sleep well that night. I was a little uncomfortable from the surgery, but mostly I was excited to have Bethany with me. She arrived the next day around noon. Ryan was in the team hotel preparing for that night's game against the Dolphins, so Sarah went to the airport to pick her up. When she walked in the door, I felt an immediate rush of strength. She came over to me and gave me a hug that spoke louder than words. It was great to know that she would be with me when the results came in. There is definitely power in the presence of someone you love.

During the next few days, I began to get my strength back. We spent the weekend in the care of the Longwells and awaited the results of the biopsy. Monday we got a call from the doctor. He said he had the results and had set up a meeting with our trainers.

Bethany and I drove to Lambeau Field to find out the news. I was wondering if it was a good sign or a bad sign that the doctor did not give me a hint as to the results. I tried to convince myself that his silence was not an issue, that he simply wasn't thinking about it at the time, and that he wanted to wait until the formal meeting. But when Bethany and I walked into the meeting room, he delivered the news.

"Josh, you're done."

12

CANCER TAKES CONTROL

My new journey had officially begun. After I broke down in the hallway leading to the players' parking lot, Bethany and I headed to the Longwells' to make the arrangements for me to go back to Oregon to begin my fight against this cancer. We found out that Oregon Health and Science University in Portland, just two hours from my home, was one of the most successful treatment facilities for testicular cancer. In fact, my chemotherapist, Dr. Nichols, had treated Lance Armstrong, the seven-time Tour de France champion. We also found out that a urologist in the same hospital was one of the foremost surgeons with regard to the next surgery I was to have. I was thankful that I was going to get the best treatment available at one of the finest facilities in the country, and I was going to be very close to home, which would make me much more comfortable during my recovery. I would be close to my family and friends, who would play a huge part in giving me the love and encouragement I needed during that difficult time.

When I first moved out to Wisconsin before training camp, I had driven my Toyota 4Runner. Now, after I began feeling quite a bit better physically, Bethany and I decided to drive back with a U-Haul trailer attached, not knowing if I would ever go back to Green Bay. In a couple days, we were packed and ready to spend the next three and a half days driving home. It was nice to have a few days of a great drive and beautiful scenery to enjoy before heading full speed into my surgery and treatments.

The drive also gave Bethany and me a chance to have candid conversations about my situation. The most difficult part of that drive home was the evening we had The Talk. I loved Bethany with all my heart, and I knew she loved me just as much, but we had to face the fact that I might not make it. It was the hardest conversation I have ever had. I wanted her to know that I loved her very much but that I wanted her to live her life to its fullest. I wanted her to feel free to get married, have children, and enjoy life with someone by her side. The thought of me leaving her behind was painful, but the thought of her feeling guilty about falling in love with someone else was even harder. I planned on beating the cancer, but if I was not going to make it, these were issues that we needed to have out in the open.

Bethany did not want to hear any of it. I couldn't believe how much she loved me and how committed she was to doing all she could to help me get through this and to take care of me. She was so selfless right from the start and showed me so much strength and commitment, I know that we will never face anything that we cannot get through together.

The day after we arrived in Oregon, I had an appointment with the urologist in charge of the surgery to remove lymph nodes from my abdominal region, where the cancer had spread. Dr. Bruce Lowe was a quiet man who had already spoken with the doctor and trainers in Green Bay. By the time of our appointment with him, he had already scheduled my surgery for the next day. The whirlwind continued.

The surgery was a lymphectomy; about 35 lymph nodes were infected with the cancer. The procedure, which was fairly invasive and required an eight-inch incision in my abdomen, went extremely well. The day after the surgery, I had a visit from Dr. Lowe. He told me that lab results showed that the nodes were infected, and I would have to have chemotherapy as soon as my body was ready.

That was very disheartening to hear. From day one, we had been holding out hope that the cancer was a seminoma. When we found out it was not, we were hopeful the cancer had not spread. But after the tests, we found out I was going to have to have chemotherapy treatments. I remember how disappointed I was, always hoping for good news when it kept coming back bad. But the doctors were extremely confident in the chemo that I was going to be using. It had been very effective in fighting this disease, and my particular situation was similar to other cases that had responded well to this treatment. That made me feel pretty good, but I was still pretty unnerved at the idea of chemo treatments. I didn't know much about it except for a few stories about how difficult it is on the patient's body.

After I was released from the hospital, I went to stay with Bethany's parents, Bob and Laura, in Eugene. I needed to be near a major hospital with a cancer center, which Eugene had, just in case of an emergency. The doctors had arranged for my chemo treatments to begin about three weeks later. I was a bit concerned about that because I knew that I was going to be getting sick from the treatments, and the thought of being sick and being weak from my surgery at the same time was a bit frightening. Because the surgery was pretty invasive, and my stomach muscles were cut, I couldn't sit up on my own and could barely walk on my own. I couldn't stand up straight, and trying to balance without using my stomach muscles made it hard to simply get from one room to the other. It was very discouraging to be so weak. I lost 45 pounds—from 225 down to 180.

Bob and Laura were absolutely amazing to me. At the time I was just the boyfriend of their daughter, but they could tell that Bethany and I were in love. They took care of me as if I were one of their own children. Not a day went by that Bob would not call from work to see if I was okay and if I needed anything. Laura worked half days at her church and was home by noon and made sure I was comfortable and had anything I needed. Bethany was living at home too and wanted to be there almost every second of the day. She wanted to be there when I was awake, and she wouldn't leave until I was asleep, when she would take time to get out of the house and have time to herself.

Bethany even slept on the floor next to the bed I was sleeping in the entire time. If I had any problems or if I needed to go to the restroom in the middle of the night, I would have to call down to Bethany to wake her, and she would get up, pick me up out of bed, and walk me to the restroom. It was humbling to be so helpless, and I learned so much about this amazing woman God had put into my life. I've never been served the way Bethany served me every second of the day during this whole ordeal. I will never forget what she did, and I have vowed to spend the rest of my life trying to show her the love and commitment she showed me. Bethany Dawn Bidwell is so much more of an amazing woman than I had ever even dreamed of, and I consider myself to be the most blessed husband on the planet.

As I started chemo, I was pretty worried about how the treatments would make me feel. I had heard horror stories and seen pictures of frail, bald, and sickly folks who had gone through chemo. Those stories and images had me a bit worried, but the treatment was not optional, and I had to suck it up and head into it knowing how effective it had been in treating my type of cancer.

I had three cycles of treatment. In each cycle, I was connected to an IV line six hours a day for five straight days. I took a few weeks off between each cycle of treatment, but every Friday, regardless of whether I was currently in a cycle of IV treatments, I also received one shot of some drugs that were part of the whole chemo regimen. The entire process lasted three months.

I learned on the first week that this was going to be difficult for me to handle. I was sick right away, and it never seemed to let up. I have always had a pretty weak stomach, which did not mesh well with the chemicals that were being poured into my body.

I was a pretty big baby. The room I was in was semicircular with ten to fifteen lounge chairs facing a big window. Doctors and nurses were stationed on the other side of the window, and televisions were mounted above it. Sitting next to Bethany and me was a sweet little older lady who had been getting a newer treatment for her cancer, and she had gotten quite a bit more than I had. This wonderful lady and her husband were there every day we were. I was so impressed with her demeanor. She had a smile on her face every day and never seemed to suffer from any of the negative effects I was experiencing. She was rock solid, and she inspired me to try as hard as I could to tough it out. I am not sure how her situation turned out, but the memory of her joy and strength will always remain fresh in my mind.

The further I progressed into my chemo treatments, the more difficulty I had not getting sick. I moved to a small private room, where I tried to sleep through as much of the day as I could. One day, as Bethany and I were in the room, we were treated with a special visitor. Lance Armstrong happened to be in town for a checkup with Dr. Nichols, who told him of my situation and asked him to stop by and give me a little encouragement. By that time, I was fully aware of who Lance was, so his visit was very special for me. I know Bethany had a great time talking with him as well after I fell asleep in the middle of his visit. He was very gracious with his time and stayed to talk to Bethany for quite a while. When I heard the encouraging report he gave Bethany and learned about his faith in Dr. Nichols and the treatment I was getting, I was extremely grateful he took the time to see us. Bethany was impressed with his passion for a second shot at life and with the drive and determination he expressed as he spoke. He clearly was not going to waste a day of his new life and wanted to make a difference in the world because of what he had experienced. His foundation has raised many millions of dollars to help fight cancer, and he has used his fame to raise people's awareness about the disease. His passion has made the difference in the world he was pushing for.

When my last treatment ended in December of 1999, Dr. Nichols told me he was sure the treatments had been effective. I would be having checkups for the next few years, but he was almost 100-percent sure I was cancer free. That was great news to hear...but would I ever be able to compete professionally again? I was so frail and weak that when I went to the mall with Bethany, I had to sit down and rest almost the entire time.

One morning Bethany and I decided to go to a local middle school to exercise on the track. Bethany ran four laps in the same amount of time I took to walk one. I had never been so weak or tired in my life. I was distressed and wondered if I would even recover enough to lead a normal life, much less compete professionally again. My goals were clear, but the journey was going to be harder than I had imagined.

◀ 13

BAD TIMING

As I was hearing the wonderful news from the doctors that I was probably going to beat this cancer, some other news started to weigh heavily on my mind. I had been diagnosed five days before NFL teams had to submit their final 53-man regular-season roster, so I didn't qualify for the NFL's insurance. Between the time of my graduation, when I had been covered by my dad's insurance, and the opening day roster, I was not covered at all. I was facing the stark reality that I was going to have to find a way to pay for all of my medical bills, which could end up totaling around $100,000. But I was thankful that I was going to be okay, so I accepted having to face this bill and decided to find a way and believe that everything would work out just fine.

Little did I know that about the same time I was thinking about all this, other people were making efforts to ease the burden I was facing. I remember the call as if it were yesterday. I was at Bob and Laura's house, still weak and frail, when Ryan Longwell called.

"Hey, Bids, how ya' feeling, buddy?"

It was great to hear from him. He called quite a bit to see how I was and to let me know he and Sarah were praying hard for me. Then he told me news that I had no idea was coming.

"Buddy, I heard about the whole insurance situation, and I got permission from the front office to go around the locker room and see if anyone wanted to donate any money to help you out. Well, pretty much all of the guys were eager to help out, and with all of the donations, we were able to raise $60,000 for you."

I couldn't believe it. I wasn't even aware any of the guys knew about the insurance situation. Hearing about what Ryan and the guys had done left me speechless. I began to tear up when I thanked Ryan and told him how much I appreciated everyone's help. I asked him to pass my thanks along to the guys and to let them know how much their generosity meant to my family and me. But Ryan wasn't finished. He said the players' wives had already organized a dinner on my behalf to raise money for me, and the team had a golf tournament scheduled to do the same.

I was blown away. I had only been in Green Bay a few months. I barely knew most of my teammates and had not even met most of their wives. Their actions demonstrated just how generous and compassionate most players and their families are in the NFL. When it was all said and done, the Packers organization raised almost $100,000 for me. Not only that, but I found out that a small school in southern Wisconsin had a penny drive and a car wash and raised a couple thousand dollars for me as well. I also received other donations from the great people of Wisconsin. In addition, someone opened an account for me in Eugene that people could donate to. In all, the total amount raised for my expenses was close to $112,000. I'm not sure of the total costs of all of my medical bills, but a lot of money was left over, and all of that was donated to the

American Cancer Society in Wisconsin. Everyone's hard work and compassion helped not only me but also many other people.

Ron Wolf, the Packers' general manager at the time, was on the forefront of seeing that I was taken care of. He worked hard, almost on a daily basis, to make sure my agent was doing all he could for me. I'm so grateful for Mr. Wolf's extra effort to help take care of me. Neither the NFL nor the team were obligated to do anything for me. My injury was unrelated to football, and I was not covered by the NFL insurance program, so without all of the work by Mr. Wolf and the Packers organization, I would have faced a much more difficult struggle. The Green Bay Packers organization is one of the most amazing in professional sports. Being a part of the team was an honor for me.

I received many letters, e-mails, and calls of encouragement from people I knew and people I had never met before. When people who had suffered as I was suffering took time to tell me how well they were doing now that they were cured, my hope grew. I learned that many people who had battled testicular cancer had since had children and were now as healthy as they had ever been. Receiving such amazing love and support has inspired me to do anything I can do to help others who are facing challenges similar to mine. I have had many opportunities to talk to other cancer patients and encourage them in much the same way that Lance and so many others encouraged me. I know what they are thinking and the questions they have. When I share my experience and encourage them, I feel as if I am doing my part to give back to all those who reached out to me.

◂ 14

SEEING LIFE
IN A WHOLE
NEW WAY

From the day I was diagnosed, I never doubted that God was in control of my life. He had always taken care of me before, and my goal was to let Him work in me during this time. I wanted to make clear to everyone I talked to that I didn't blame God for my cancer. I was certain that God did not make me sick, but He knew, even before I was born, that at 23 years of age, I would be diagnosed with testicular cancer. That helped me realize that He had been spending the past 23 years preparing me to be able to handle this situation. That was why I was never going to ask God, *Why me?* However, I would ask Him, *What is it that You want from me?* Knowing that God's Word tells me He will never leave me nor forsake me and that He wants only the best for me helped me to rest my spirit in Him the entire time.

As I faced my diagnosis, I thought again about the day in my sophomore year in high school when I gave my life to Jesus. I had always believed that heaven and hell existed, and I wanted so badly to know I would go to heaven when I died. The day I gave my heart to

Jesus was the day I finally knew I would spend eternity with God in heaven when I died. And the day I was told I had cancer brought the reality of my own mortality to the forefront of my mind.

Few of us ever really contemplate the fact that we will all die eventually. Or we think it will happen when we are old and gray, not when we are 23. Facing this reality while I was so young, I was immediately grateful that God saved me that day in high school. That was the ultimate reason I gave my life to Jesus: When I die, by cancer or old age, I will know my sins are forgiven in Christ. That decision never seemed more real to me than on the day I was diagnosed.

My first real fear was not of dying. My biggest fear was of all the uncertainty. I had no control over what was going to happen to me. My life was out of my hands and in the doctors' and ultimately in God's. I didn't know what tomorrow would hold, and that terrified me. I had spent my whole life operating under the premise that if *I* worked hard and did what *I* was supposed to, then *I* would have a shot to achieve my dreams. But my formula didn't work in this situation. God was noticeably absent in this equation even though I would insert Him occasionally when I felt I needed to.

I could have done everything the doctors ordered, and it still might not have mattered—as was true for a young man in Arizona whom I met through a mutual friend. He was only 18, and his cancer was in exactly the same stage mine had been. He did everything I had done to treat the cancer, but before he knew it, the cancer reappeared, and he died just a few weeks later. One week we were talking about how excited we were that his treatments seemed to work so well, the next week I heard he was sick again, and he died just a short time later.

Earlier, each day had seemed to bring more bad news my way. Every time I was given a best-case scenario, it was followed by more bad news. At the first diagnosis, we hoped the tumor was just a seminoma and I would be fine in a couple weeks, but then we found out that was not the case and that the cancer was very aggressive. After the lymphectomy, we hoped the cancer hadn't spread, but after the surgery we learned it had and that I needed chemotherapy treatments.

I kept holding out hope, but the news kept getting worse, and that made it difficult for me to let go of my fears and rest in God. The reality of my eternal security was a huge comfort, but my innate desire to fight for my life was being suppressed by the helplessness I felt about what tomorrow would hold. But God blessed me with many wonderful brothers and sisters in Christ. As they encouraged me, I slowly learned to trust God each step of the way.

I recall sitting in my usual spot on Bob and Laura's couch, bald headed, 45 pounds underweight, too weak to get up on my own, and wondering if I would ever have a strong body again. One day, Kevin Tommasini called and said God had put me on his heart, and he wanted to know how I was feeling. I told him what I was struggling with and that I was getting a bit discouraged about my physical progress.

His call was such a godsend. He pointed me to an amazing portion of Scripture that God had shown him just a few days before. The passage, 2 Corinthians 12:7-10, tells the story of the apostle Paul being given a thorn in his flesh that tormented him. This is widely interpreted to have been an actual physical ailment. Kevin pointed out that Paul prayed three times for God to take it away, but God did not. Rather, God said to Paul, "My grace is sufficient for you, for my power is made perfect in weakness." Listen to what Paul said after God told him this: "Therefore I will boast all the more gladly about my weaknesses, so that Christ's power may rest on me. That is why, for Christ's sake, I delight in weaknesses, in insults, in hardships, in persecutions, in difficulties. For when I am weak, then I am strong."

Kevin encouraged me to work as hard as I could to get my strength back but also to rest on God's strength and sovereignty in my life. He reminded me that God was doing something amazing in and through me even though I could not see it just yet. When I got off the phone I went right to that passage and read it again. I prayed at that moment that God would give me the same understanding in my situation that He gave to Paul in his time of trial.

Countless other people gave me encouragement from the first day to the last. I received hundreds of letters, e-mails, and calls. I had a lot of visitors and met a lot of new people who blessed me with their inspiring stories of success. One day, as I headed up to Portland for a chemo treatment, I saw a sign just off the interstate that read, "Please pray for Josh Bidwell." I'm sure thousands of people drove by and read that sign and wondered, *Who's Josh Bidwell?* But I'm also sure that some of them said a quick prayer for me. To this day, I haven't met the person who was responsible for that sign, but I was touched and grateful for the heartfelt gesture. A little encouragement goes a long way, but prayer reaches into eternity.

While I was in the hospital recovering from the second surgery, I received a call from my high school football coach, Mr. Taylor. He happens to be a very funny person—sometimes I think he could make a rock laugh. He called just to find out how I was. He knew the next few months were going to be very challenging for me, and he gave me a quote from Mother Teresa that made me laugh but encouraged me as well: "I know God will not give me anything I cannot handle. I just wish that He did not trust me so much."

Mr. Taylor, in his usual humorous way, taught me a great lesson that day. He reminded me that God was in total control and had actually entrusted me with this terrible situation. Just as I decided to do from the beginning, I resolved again to use every second of this situation to show the love of Christ to all who would come into contact with me. If Mother Teresa could endure a lifetime of hardships and still show the world that God is in control and loves us, I could embrace my own affliction and do my best to do the same.

Now that I am well, I have had many opportunities to do just that. One of my former college teammates and I had an encounter where I applied the same principle Mother Teresa illustrated in her quote. I had just started working out with Coach Radcliffe in the U of O weight room. I was so weak, I was only able to do one set of eight or ten reps with almost no weight on the machine. My total workout time took about 20 minutes before I was too exhausted to go any further.

I ran into my friend in the hallway after a strenuous workout. I was still bald and still 45 pounds underweight, and I still had to walk very slowly because my body was so weak and a bit unstable. I could see in his eyes that looking at me was hard for him. He and I had played five years together, and if the roles were reversed, I would have had a hard time looking at him as well. He knew me as one of the strongest guys on the team just months before, and now he had to see me in this state. No doubt he probably thought I might be bitter at my situation.

He asked me a lot of questions, which quickly led to me talking about what God was doing in my life. He was not a Christian, but he could see that my faith in Jesus was real and active in my life. He always knew I was a Christian, but now he saw my faith grow in the midst of this trial, just as I had seen the apostle Paul's faith grow. At the end of our conversation, I told him that getting cancer had been the biggest blessing I had ever had in my life because I could see God more clearly and feel Him more deeply than ever before.

I would later hear from a friend of mine that my comment had a huge impact on him. He could hardly believe that I could call my cancer a blessing. He said he wanted to have that type of strength in his own life. I am not sure if he has ever given his life to Jesus, but I know God used me that day to show him just how amazing He is in the lives of those who love Him.

Many people helped me get as much out of this experience as I could. I was so grateful for my family and friends who were constantly encouraging me. That was exactly what I needed. Bethany was my biggest and most constant encourager. She was with me almost every second of the day, supporting me when I was down and listening to me when I needed to talk. I cannot express how much more I fell in love with her during that time. The love, commitment, and selflessness she showed still amazes me. She would later say that she could handle the whole situation with such strength only because of God's grace. She explained it as "the peace of God, which transcends all understanding" that the Bible speaks of in the book of Philippians. She had a peace and a strength that was not her own, and I needed that to help strengthen me when times were getting hard.

I didn't enjoy not being able to do anything for myself for so long and having to rely on Bethany to help me with even the simplest of tasks. But that led to the biggest lesson I learned through the entire experience. I've already mentioned my fear of the unknown. I shared earlier that my life consisted of working as hard as I could and doing what I needed to do to take control, to achieve my goals. The problem was that I was not giving God every part of my life. God wants us to yield *everything* we have to Him. He wants to be in control of it all. As a man, that was hard for me to accept. I wanted then, and I still do at times, to feel in control and in charge of my life. I knew I could not control some things, and I had no problem asking God to take charge of those areas in my life. But as for everything else, I wanted that for myself.

For the longest time, my formula in my life seemed to work just fine. In high school, I had done what I was supposed to and earned a college scholarship. In college, I did what I was supposed to and earned a shot at playing in the NFL. I was at the top of my life's dreams when all of a sudden it all came crashing down. The worst part about it was that it all happened outside of my control. I couldn't have prevented this from happening, and I couldn't guarantee anything in the days to come. God had finally gotten everything from me. He was in complete control and had my complete attention.

I was able to fully understand what it meant to submit everything to the Lord. Just as I had to rely on Bethany for the most menial of tasks (like getting out of bed at night to go to the restroom), God was teaching me to rely on Him for everything. No part of my life was too big or too small to give to Him. I'm like every other man on the planet; I don't like to watch TV if I don't have the remote right next to me. I like to be the one in the driver's seat. I'm just not comfortable until I feel in charge and take control. God made it as clear as day as He spoke to my heart that He wants to be in control, and if I allow Him to, He will take me places I could never go under my own power.

◀ 15

GOD GIVES ME A
SECOND CHANCE

When my cancer treatments officially ended at the beginning of December 1999, I was in rough shape physically, but my relationship with Bethany had never been better. The girl of my dreams had become the most important person in my life, and I wasn't about to let her go. As the twentieth century came to a close, I asked Bethany to marry me. We had a romantic dinner at a very nice restaurant in Eugene on December 31. At that dinner I expressed to Bethany just how much she meant to me and how incredibly grateful I was for the way she sacrificed so much while taking care of me. I told her I didn't want to live my life without her, and as I got down on my knee, teary eyed and overwhelmed with emotion, I asked the most amazing woman I have ever known to be my wife. God had shown us that we were, unquestionably, meant to be together. She was a source of strength and encouragement that I needed on a daily basis, and her love and support helped drive me as I started to work my body back into shape.

Bethany and I were married on June 17, 2000, just before the beginning of the season. I had been living and training in Green Bay for the majority of the spring, so Bethany was left back home to plan the entire wedding without my help at all. Fortunately, she has an amazing family, and they were incredibly generous with their time and helped her with all the planning. Many women would be upset if their future husbands were not around to help plan the wedding, but Bethany, her mom, and her aunt Gail seemed to be glad I was not around to be in the way!

Needless to say, they all did an amazing job. The wedding was exactly what Bethany had always envisioned, and the entire day flowed without a hitch. While I was growing up, I never envisioned what my wedding would be like (as I have learned that all girls do), but I did often dream of what my wife would be like. As I took my place on the platform and saw Bethany walking down the aisle toward me, looking more beautiful than ever, I realized that I was marrying a more amazing woman than I could have hoped for.

Bethany had been such a source of strength and comfort for me during the most difficult time in my life. I was excited and comforted to know that she was coming to Green Bay with me as I worked to attain my NFL dream once again.

The Packers had told me I would have another shot at the punting position when I was healthy, but I had a long way to go to get there. The University of Oregon football staff did all they could to help me out and get me back into shape—especially Coach Radcliffe. I have considered him to be one of the best strength coaches out there, and I owe him a lot for his efforts in getting me back into shape.

It was not easy for me to get back to working out when I was so weak and discouraged. My workouts at first lasted less than a half an hour. I was used to working much longer than that. The fact that I could hardly lift any weight made it all the more discouraging for me. Coach Rad made sure I remained patient and stuck to the plan he drew up for me. At times I felt a little bit like the Karate Kid when Mr. Miyagi made Daniel do seemingly meaningless tasks. Coach Rad did not always show me where I was going week by week in my workouts, so I just trusted that he had the right plan and knew what I needed to do to get ready to compete again by training camp.

I quickly found out I could regain my strength much faster than I attained it in the beginning. My strength in the weight room came pretty quickly after just a few weeks. By March, my body weight was getting pretty close to normal, and after three months, I was feeling as strong as ever. I was on my way, and I knew it. By the time training camp had arrived, I was once again eager to realize the dream I had been so close to the year before.

Still, I was fighting an uphill battle. During the off-season, the Packers had fired the head coach and his entire staff. The team hired a brand-new head coach and an entirely new coaching staff, including a new special-teams coach who clearly did not want to have a rookie punter. Rookie punters experience growing pains: dealing with nerves, handling the pressures of big situations in games, and facing the probability of poor kicks at crucial points in a game. A lot of coaches would rather have a veteran punter who they know can overcome those challenges. That was the new special-teams coach's perspective, so I had a lot of work to do to get my job back.

I understood that coaches have as much pressure to keep their jobs as players do, and they are often on the hot seat because of a player whom they are responsible for. But it was hard for me to handle the pressure of trying to achieve my own personal goals while dealing with the mental strain of feeling as though my coach was wanting so badly to get rid of me.

By the way, this same coach and I are friends to this day and have a lot of respect for each other and what we have been able to accomplish in our professional careers and in life. Coaches and players sometimes have to overcome side issues to make it in this business whether we like it or not. I think we both handled our situation very well, and that is why we were able to have the success we had together there.

Earlier in the off-season, before moving back for training camp, I traveled to Green Bay for a couple minicamps. A minicamp is simply a weeklong practice session. The practices are not in full pads, but they are run the same way as a normal practice during the season. At the end of the week, I would travel back home to Oregon. At my first minicamp, I knew I was fighting an uphill battle not only with my new special-teams coach but with other punters as well. The NFL does not give free rides. As soon as I arrived, I noticed that two other punters were there to compete against me for the one and only punting job. We kicked every day, and every single kick was measured and recorded so the coaches could keep track of who was performing the best. We had no days off. Every day I headed out to practice, knowing that all my punts had to be nearly perfect so I could outshine the other guys. Obviously, they had the same goal. Our special-teams coach scrutinized every detail of every aspect of our performance.

From the start of training camp to the end, I had a lot to prove. The team brought in two more punters to compete for the job, bringing the total to five. In the middle of this high-pressure situation, I was made to alter an aspect of my punting, and the change actually took a bit away from my abilities rather than maximizing them. My special-teams coach told me that once I caught the ball,

I took too much time to kick it. The ideal hand-to-foot time is around 1.3 seconds, and I was between that and 1.45 seconds. The coach's changes to my punting approach felt unnatural. I wasn't able to catch the ball and kick it rhythmically, and punting the ball became much more difficult than it had to be. However, I was not in a position to talk back or plead my case, so I just kept quiet and tried to do what I was told.

I stayed very focused and eventually emerged as the front-runner to win the spot. Every day we had two practices and punted in both of them. That takes a huge toll on a kicker's leg. It's like having a baseball pitcher throw full speed every day, twice a day. After a while, our legs were getting very sore and very tired. However, we all had to continue, knowing what was on the line with every ball we punted.

By the time we got to our first preseason game, I was number one on the depth chart with just one other guy left on the roster as competition. I was more driven than ever to do all I could to get back the dream that just a few months prior felt so distant.

I will never forget my first game back. It was a preseason game in Green Bay against the New York Jets. As a preseason game, it didn't count for anything in the books. But for me, it was an emotional experience that seemed a bit surreal the whole night. When I ran out on the field with Ryan to warm up during the team introductions, I just stood in the middle of the field, looking around and taking it all in. I had made it at least that far.

Ryan hugged me and said, "Congratulations, buddy! Can you believe you're here, right now, about to play this game? What an amazing year you just had! God really is great, isn't He?"

He was right. I couldn't believe God had just taken me through all of that and brought me to that point, in historic Lambeau Field, about to play in an NFL game again. I had only two punts that day, but they were both good punts and got the job done for the game. The preseason continued to go well for me. I was not breaking any records, but I was punting solidly, and by the time the final cuts came, I got the call telling me that the team had released the other punter. I was once again the starting punter for the Green Bay Packers.

My first regular season as an NFL player was full of ups and downs.

I did not play as well as I would have liked. I only averaged 38.5 yards per punt that season, but I also had a lot to be thankful for. I did very well in a few games, and I never had a punt blocked. Parts of that season are still a bit of a blur for me. I worked so hard and endured so much adversity, I really didn't get to fully appreciate that I was living my lifelong dream.

Still, I took time in every game to watch all the great players on my team and those we played against. I was actually playing in games with and against some of my all-time heroes. That surreal experience took a bit of time to get accustomed to.

Interestingly enough, Darren Bennett, the punter for the San Diego Chargers, whom I had worked out with in college, had followed my progress through college and my misfortunes in the pros. We had not spoken for nearly four years since our short week of working out together, but he had continued to send me messages of encouragement through my grandpa's friend during my days at the University of Oregon. He was one of the first people to send an encouraging message to me when the news of my cancer diagnosis was released.

One of the highlights of my career occurred the first time we played against the San Diego Chargers, where Darren was in his final year with the team. Before the game, a lot of the players like to head out to the field to run around and chat with some of the guys on the other team. As soon as I got out on the field that day, I felt a tap on my shoulder, and sure enough, it was Darren! When we talked on the field, I realized with amazement how closely he had kept tabs on my college career. He took a lot of pride in my success and the fact that I had made it to the NFL. He had become one of my sports heroes, and I was flattered to hear his compliments on my career to that point.

Competing against Darren as a peer in the NFL was a tremendous thrill. After the game, he reiterated that he was proud to see that I had beat cancer and made it back to the NFL. His words meant a lot to me. I respected him so much and owed a lot of my success to him, so to have him hold me in such high regard as a competitor was a great honor. That small bit of encouragement and his compliments made my comeback all the more special to me.

A few other games still stick in my mind. One was a Monday night game—one of my first. Monday night games are a lot of fun, and they are very different from regular games on Sunday because 40 million people watch on Monday nights. The buzz before the game is hard to ignore as we wait all day long for the game to finally arrive. When it does, the game experience is unique. The stadium is a bit louder, the fans are more energetic, and the players seem to have a little more in their tank.

This particular game was at home against the Minnesota Vikings, and the weather was awful—windy and rainy the entire game. It was a tight game all the way down to the end, and the Vikings were moving into field goal range. With time about to expire, Minnesota lined up for what would be the game-winning field goal, but when the ball was snapped to the holder, he dropped it. The wet, slick ball slipped right through his fingers, and the kicker had to fall on it. The clock ran out on that play, and we went into overtime.

We won the coin toss and elected to receive the kick. We ran about four or five plays before being forced into a third and long situation. If we didn't get a first down, I would have to punt the ball back to the Vikings. I was getting pretty nervous about punting that night because we were facing a very strong wind and it was absolutely pouring down rain. Little did I know that one of the NFL's greatest plays was about to occur. Brett took the snap, dropped back, and let it fly. The ball flew high and far, down the right side of the field in the direction of one of our star receivers, Antonio Freeman, who had a defender there right with him. They both went up for the ball at the same time. They tipped it up into the air as they fell to the ground.

Antonio hit the ground first, the defender landed on top of him, and the ball bounced off of the back of the defender. Antonio reached out and caught the ball from behind his back with one hand. The defender slid past the play, and the safety overran Antonio as he got up and ran into the end zone for the game-winning score. The play was amazing and actually won a major sports award as the most exciting sports play of the year. I can still hear the roar of the crowd when the referees signaled for the touchdown. But they were twice as loud when the referee revealed that the instant replay confirmed that he did, in fact, catch the ball and that the game-winning touchdown would stand. Many consider that to be one of the greatest endings to a Monday Night Football game ever. I'm thankful to have had the opportunity to be there and to play in that game.

The Packers played well that entire season, and we were right in the middle of the playoff race. By the last game of the year, we knew what needed to happen for us to make the playoffs. We had to beat the Broncos, the St. Louis Rams had to beat the New Orleans Saints, and the Detroit Lions had to beat the lowly Chicago Bears.

We were routing the Broncos late in the fourth quarter, and our scoreboard flashed the scores of other games that were playing at that same time. The Rams had just beaten the Saints. Only one more outcome, and we were in: As long as the Lions beat the Bears, we were going to be in the playoffs. We won our game and headed for our locker room not knowing what had happened in the Detroit-Chicago game. By the time we were all in the locker room the results were in. Paul Edinger, the kicker for the Chicago Bears, had just kicked a 55-yard field goal to win the game as time expired. Detroit had been leading by one or two points at the time, so if Edinger hadn't kicked that unlikely field goal, we would have been in the playoffs. As it was, our season was over at that moment, and my first season as an NFL player was officially completed.

In so many ways, I was blessed to have played a season in the NFL. The Green Bay Packers organization had been absolutely amazing. Ron Wolf, the rest of the administration, the coaches, the trainers, the players and their wives, the Green Bay fans, and most importantly Ryan and Sarah showed me so much love and support that I still don't think I could ever repay them for all they did that year. None of them were obligated to do what they did, especially the organization.

The team could easily have wished me well and sent me on my way. They had a season to focus on, which takes an enormous amount of time and effort, but still made sure I was getting all I needed to beat my cancer. No one would have faulted the team if they had decided to sever ties with me, to rid themselves of the distraction, and to move on with trying to win a championship that year. I certainly would not have held a grudge if that were the case. I'm so appreciative to them all for what they did for me, knowing that football is important but that life is always more important than the game. They held strong to that conviction and have motivated me to devote the rest of my life to doing the same in any way I can.

The next season, I was determined to improve. I finished near the bottom of the NFC standings statistically, and I worked hard studying my game film and working on my technique so I could give myself every opportunity to get better. I also made a decision to go back to my old and comfortable approach, and I worked hard to reduce my hand-to-foot time. I knew that getting a great punt off was better than getting a bad punt off fast. I decided that the most important thing I could work on was my consistency in punting a great ball every time, even if that meant that my hand-to-foot time wasn't much below 1.3 seconds. For the entire off season,

I did just that. I worked on drill after drill to get myself comfortable with working fast and building consistency. That consistency allowed me to win the job, hands down, from the competition that was brought in the next season.

Once again, I was not given the job; I was expected to earn it by outperforming whomever the team brought in to compete with me. This time, they brought in a veteran punter named Tom Hutton, who had a stellar career with the Philadelphia Eagles for a few years. Tom and I became good friends during training camp as we competed. He was at the end of his career but was still a good punter and had the résumé to back it up. He was the veteran my special-teams coach wanted all along. However, I was a different player at this training camp, and it showed. Tom was a consistent punter, but he was not as strong as I was. With the dramatic improvements I made to my consistency and the power I was able to maximize, there was not much competition happening between us. Tom even confided in me that he called his agent after the first week of camp and asked why he was even there. His agent admitted that Tom didn't have a chance against me, and he wondered why the Packers were not more supportive of me as a player.

That was the type of encouragement I needed all along. Such great compliments from an accomplished veteran meant a lot and made me feel even more confident in myself. That confidence stayed with me, and that season would prove to be my best season as a Packer. My average increased from 38.6 yards per punt my first year to 42.5 yards per punt the next. I had the second-best net average in Packers team history. The work I had done in the off season and my decision to revert back to my initial approach helped me to feel a lot more comfortable, and that translated into a lot more confidence. I was one of the best that season in the NFC and was voted as an alternate on the Pro Bowl team that year. Unfortunately, only one punter goes to Hawaii, and there are no backups. The only way I would get a chance to go to the Pro Bowl that year was if the person ahead of me was not able to make it for some reason, and as much as I would have liked that to happen, it did not. Being voted near the top was an honor, but going to Hawaii that year would have been nice.

That season we did much better as a team as well. We finished the season with a tremendous 12 and 4 record and a spot in the play-offs. In my first playoff game, we played the San Francisco 49ers at Lambeau Field. The 49ers held a 7–6 lead at halftime, but we came back in the second half to earn a 25–15 victory. That was a pretty big deal for me. No Green Bay Packer team had ever lost a home playoff game, and I did not want to be on the team that ended that streak.

Playoff games definitely feel much more intense than regular season games. Every player knows we will win or go home. Every team's first goal for each season is to get into the playoffs so they can have a shot at the Super Bowl. I felt that desperate passion on the field. I resolved to do my part to extend our season one game closer to getting to the Super Bowl. By the end of the 49ers game, I had set the bar high for my future games. We won the game convincingly, and I had the game of my life. I had an identical net and gross average of 47.8 yards per punt in the game. That was the second-highest net punting average in a postseason game in NFL history and the highest in any NFL game in more than 45 years. I was voted by the NFL as the Special Teams Player of the Week for my efforts.

However, the joy was short-lived because a week later on the road in St. Louis, our season came to a crashing end as Brett Favre had a nightmarish six-interception game in a 45–17 loss to the Rams.

That season was my personal best to date, and the next two seasons went almost as well for me. We finished each of the next two seasons with a playoff spot, but in the 2003 playoffs, the unthinkable happened. We suffered the first-ever playoff home loss in

Packers history. Our battle against the Atlanta Falcons was close all the way to the end, but we came up a bit too short.

Amazingly, the same thing happened the next season, my final season with the Packers. In our playoff game against the Philadelphia Eagles, we jumped out to a 14–0 lead by the end of the first quarter. The Eagles clawed their way back into the game, tying it at 14 in the fourth quarter. We retook the lead at 17–14 when Ryan kicked a field goal with just over four minutes left. Our defense put the Eagles in a huge hole, and we needed just one more stop on a fourth and 26, but our defense allowed a miracle first down, allowing the Eagles to tie the game and force it into overtime. In overtime we threw a quick interception that set the Eagles up for a chip shot game-winning field goal that ended our season with a heartbreaking 20–17 loss.

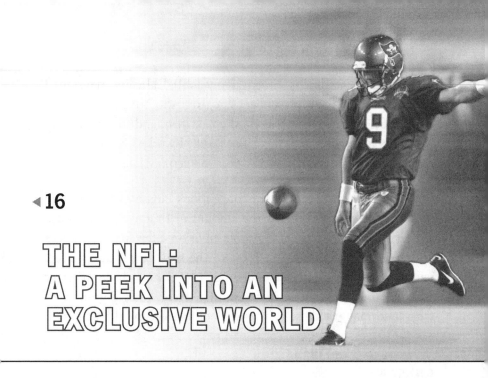

16

THE NFL:
A PEEK INTO AN
EXCLUSIVE WORLD

When I was a young boy, I dreamed of meeting any professional athlete, but mostly I wanted to meet a real NFL player. Having been in the NFL for a few years now, the novelty that it used to hold has worn off just a bit, but I try to always keep myself aware of my childhood enchantment with professional players when I am talking to people who want to know about life in the NFL. People often ask me the same questions, but each time is the first time for the individuals I meet, so I always try to help feed their excitement.

One of the most common questions I get is, "What's it like to be in the NFL?" It's hard to communicate how it feels to be a part of something this special, something so many people dream of but so few get a chance to experience. All I can say is that it feels surreal to be a part of this league and play this game against so many famous players—and get paid to do it! So many players don't make it each year, and even more players are waiting in the wings to get their shot at realizing their own dream of playing in this great league.

(Sometimes that shot is aimed at my job!) I already mentioned that more than 1400 players get cut from the NFL each year. A lot of those players will try again the next year, and the graduating college players enter into the mix as well. I worked hard to get to this level, and I work hard every year to keep my job.

One of the most common misconceptions fans have concerning professional football regards the amount of time we put into preparing for each game. Some people envision a few short practices and a game on Sunday. But most of the regular position players endure a grinding daily schedule. Each team has a little different schedule, but they are all pretty similar. Here is just a glimpse of what a normal weekly schedule will look like during the season:

MONDAY

▶ **8:00 a.m. to 11:00 a.m.:** strength, conditioning, and treatment

This is when players lift weights, run, and receive treatment for injuries they may have suffered in the previous game or may have already had. The sooner you can get your training and film study in, the sooner you can get home and enjoy the rest of the day off.

▶ **11:15 a.m. to 12:15 p.m.:** special-teams meeting

Here we watch every special-teams play from the previous game. There are 11 players on each special-teams play, and we review each player's performance on each play. And the film is taken from two different angles, so we watch each play more than 22 times.

▶ **12:15 p.m. to 12:30 p.m.:** team meeting

This meeting is quick. Our head coach will make brief comments about the positives and negatives of the previous game.

He will also make a few comments about the next team we are going to play.

▶ **12:30 p.m. to 2:00 p.m.:** quick lunch and then watch film by position

> During this meeting, position players meet with their position coaches to watch every play from the previous game. For example, all receivers meet with the receivers coach; all running backs meet with their coach, and so forth.

TUESDAY

Tuesday is typically the day off for all teams. However, most players will come in for a few hours to lift, run, and watch more film to get a head start on the game plan for the next opponent. Each of these players has to learn new plays, new defensive schemes, and new ways to attack the next opponent. Many players say they need to go in on Tuesdays to make sure they get all the information they need for the next game.

WEDNESDAY

▶ **7:00 a.m. to 9:00 a.m.:** strength, conditioning, and treatment
▶ **8:00 a.m. to 8:45 a.m.:** quarterbacks and special-teams meetings
▶ **8:45 a.m. to 8:50 a.m.:** team meeting
▶ **8:50 a.m. to 10:35 a.m.:** position meetings

> At this meeting, players watch film of the next opponent and to install the plays that have been put in to run against them.

▶ **10:45 a.m. to 11:35 a.m.:** walk-through

> During the walk-through, the offense sets up and runs their

plays against a mock defense while the defense does the same against a practice offense on the adjacent practice field. This is all done at a very slow pace to give each player an "on the field" look at what they just watched on film during the previous meeting.

▶ **11:35 a.m. to 12:20 p.m.:** lunch

▶ **12:50 a.m. to 3:15 p.m.:** practice

Practices are pretty much the same every day. We begin with each position running a few warm-up drills with their position coaches and talking over some of the plays they will be working on that day. The practice then moves into a rhythm of alternating between offensive emphasis and defensive emphasis periods, much the same as we did in college. Midway through each practice, we spend 20 minutes or so on special teams, kicking field goals and punting as a team. This is virtually the same as the format we had in college.

▶ **3:45 p.m.:** postpractice meetings

These meetings will vary in length for each position. Most players will take their playbooks and DVDs of the next opponent home for extra study.

THURSDAY

Thursday's schedule is identical to Wednesday's.

FRIDAY

▶ **7:00 a.m. to 9:00 a.m.:** strength, conditioning, and treatment

▶ **8:00 a.m. to 9:00 a.m.:** quarterbacks and special-teams meetings

▶ **9:00 a.m. to 9:05 a.m.:** team meeting

- **9:05 a.m. to 10:20 a.m.:** position meetings
- **10:30 a.m. to 10:50 a.m.:** walk-through
- **10:50 a.m. to 12:10 p.m.:** practice

  Players usually have Friday afternoon off, but some stick around to watch film.

SATURDAY

- **7:00 a.m. to 9:00 a.m.:** strength, conditioning, and treatment
- **8:00 a.m. to 9:00 a.m.:** quarterbacks and special-teams meetings
- **9:00 a.m. to 9:05 a.m.:** team meeting
- **9:05 a.m. to 9:50 a.m.:** position meetings
- **10:00 a.m. to 10:30 a.m.:** walk-through

  This walk-through is very quick and is designed to provide one last look at a few plays the team will run, including a few special plays for that week's game.

After this walk-through, if we have a home game, we have the rest of the day off until 7:00 p.m., when we report to our team hotel for more meetings and to check into our rooms. Even for home games, we are required to stay in the team hotel. This ensures that no one does anything silly the night before the game and that everyone gets enough rest so they are ready to play the next day.

If we have a road game, we are off until 1:30 p.m., when we report to our practice facility, load up on buses as a team, and go to our chartered plane to fly to the city of our next game. After the game, we are at the stadium for about an hour and a half. Then we head straight to the airport to load up and fly home.

Home games are pretty straightforward. All players are required to be at the stadium no later than two hours before the game. That ensures that no players get stuck in traffic and are late for the game. It also gives the coaches enough time to talk to players one last time about the game.

When I am asked what it is like to be in the NFL, I try to convey that it is a job. Fans are often surprised to hear that we do as much as we do each week during the season. The game has become so complicated and the talent level so great that each player has to do whatever he can to prepare himself physically and mentally to compete. I have seen some pretty good players get fired because they didn't think they needed to work hard off the field to get better. It takes a lot more than physical talent to make it in this league—much to the surprise of the average fan. In every great touchdown pass play, in every long run or interception, a great player executed a game plan that allowed him to make that great play. If that player didn't know where he was supposed to be, he wouldn't have made the play. Playing in the NFL is a lot of fun, but it's a lot more work and pressure than I could have imagined when I was a kid dreaming of making it here.

ROUGHING THE KICKER

The average spectator never sees some aspects of NFL games. I've had the privilege of playing long enough to see and hear what happens on the field during games. Everyone knows a lot of talking happens between players on the same team and between players on opposing teams, but fans rarely know what they are saying. I would like to make it clear that a lot of what is said definitely needs to stay on the field. Players sometimes exchange unkind and inappropriate words in the heat of battle. But sometimes certain players will say something funny—especially Brett Favre.

Brett once wore a mic during a Monday night game in Green Bay when Pat Morita (Mr. Miyagi from the movie *The Karate Kid*) was on our sideline. That night, *SportsCenter* played a small segment featuring Brett's comments throughout that game. During one time-out at a pretty crucial point in the game, Brett was standing in the huddle with the offense. But rather than talking to the offense and trying to encourage them to focus on putting a great scoring drive together, Brett took the opportunity to talk about how small Mr. Miyagi was in real life and to make a few comments about his ponytail. It was hilarious! No doubt Brett was focused on the task at hand, but he is a kid at heart and often takes time to get his jokes in—whether they are good or bad!

Similar situations will occur between players and referees. Obviously referees are under fire the entire game from both teams and their coaches. When they make a call that goes one way, one team is happy and the other is not, and when they make a call that goes the other way, the other team is upset. Theirs is truly a thankless job.

I have had my share of conversations with referees. I've never been so angry that I yelled at a ref, but I have had to plead my case about a call or a lack of a call. For example, as a punter, I am one of the most protected players on the field. When I am kicking the ball, no player from the opposing team is allowed to touch me unless he touches the ball first. If a defender just barely runs into me, an official calls a five-yard penalty. If we are closer than five yards to a first down, the penalty results in us getting a first down, and our offense has another chance to score. If a defender really clobbers me without touching the ball, an official will call a 15-yard penalty and an automatic first down.

As you might well imagine, as long as I am okay, it is better for me to make it seem as though I was hit hard enough to warrant a 15-yard penalty. Some might call it cheating, but I call it gamesmanship! Either way, it is an attempt at deception on my part for sure.

My first lesson in the art of "flopping" came in my first year. I kicked the ball away and was immediately hit pretty hard by an opposing player. My instincts at the time told me to not look like a wimp and to stay on my feet as best I could. So after getting spun around and losing my balance, rather than just falling down and groaning (supposedly in pain), I fought to stay on my feet as best I could. A ref threw a flag on the play, but because I fought to stay on my feet, he decided the defender didn't hit me hard enough to warrant a 15-yard penalty. In actuality, he hit me plenty hard enough for the stiffer penalty. When the call was made and I got to the sideline, I was immediately greeted by our special-teams coach, who was livid that I didn't do my part to draw the 15-yard penalty. I learned then that whether I was hit hard or barely hit at all, my duty was to spin, contort, and fall to the ground, groaning as if I had been hit by a truck. The sheer agony that I portray as I lay there, seemingly an invalid, wrecked from the violence of the illegal and irresponsible actions of the opposing player, will convince the referee that the only appropriate consequence for that player's despicable action is the stiffest of penalties—the 15-yard penalty and an automatic first down.

I am ashamed to say that a few times in my career—a very few— I have succumbed to the peer pressure from my teammates and coaches and have flopped after a collision that probably wasn't bad enough to warrant more than a five-yard penalty. However, because of my incredible acting skills and the hard lesson I learned my rookie year, I was able to give the perception that my life was nearing its end because of the violence I endured on that illegal play, and we were awarded the 15-yard penalty and a first down.

Those situations do occur, but they are very rare. A few years ago, an opposing rusher barely touched me as I booted the ball away. I immediately fell to the ground, trying to draw the bigger penalty. However, this was such a light hit that I probably exerted more effort falling than I would have simply catching my balance and shaking it off. As I got up and saw the flag lying nearby, I knew a ref was about to make the call. Normally I would get up and go to the referee and plead my case as to why he should call for the stiffer of the two penalties. But in this particular case, Ed Hochuli, one of the NFL's best referees, approached me before I could say a word.

"Don't even try it, Bidwell. You were barely hit, and we both know it. It's only a five-yard penalty."

Usually I would argue for the sake of arguing, but in this case it was painfully obvious that he was right. I was barely touched. I couldn't hold back a sheepish grin. He smiled back and said, "You already knew that though, didn't you?"

I laughed and nodded as I told him I'd worked hard enough trying to draw the five-yard penalty and that I didn't want to be too greedy.

UNIQUE OPPORTUNITIES

The NFL has provided me with two opportunities to meet the president of the United States! The first time I met him, President Bush made a surprise visit to one of our practices in Green Bay. Ryan and I found out the day before that he was going to be there, and we arranged to have our wives there, hoping they would get to meet him as well. We didn't know that our head coach would be extremely irritated that we did this, but even now, Ryan and I know it was well worth his heartache.

It was a pretty cool experience. Near the end of practice, while the whole team was running drills, we all noticed a bit of a commotion near the indoor practice facility at the end of the field. Before we knew it, real-life "men in black" came walking around the corner, followed by a huge entourage of media personnel, other officials, and of course, George W. Bush. This was actually a week or two before he was first elected, so at the time he was not yet the president, but meeting him was pretty cool anyway. As he and his entourage made their way to where the team was, we stopped our practice and waited to hear a few words from him and possibly get a chance to converse with him a bit. As he made his way toward the team, our head coach greeted him and asked if he wanted to say anything to all of us standing there. Of course, he said he would love to, and he addressed us with a simple bit of encouragement. He wanted us to know how much the entire country looked up to us as professional athletes, and he encouraged us to work hard to be great examples to kids and to be people that our fans could be proud to root for. His comments were not very long, but he spoke well and made a good point.

At the end of his little bit of encouragement, he thanked us for our time and attention. As we all clapped and expressed our gratitude, he encouraged us to vote for him in the upcoming election. One of his big campaign points was that he was going to lower the highest tax bracket, so as we were all clapping, one of the players in the back said, "Yeah, I'll vote for you...as long as you're not lying about lowering my taxes!" That got a pretty big laugh out of everyone—even Mr. Bush, who replied, "You just vote for me and keep making the kind of money you're making, and we'll both be fine!"

After goofing around with the players and playing catch for a moment with Brett Favre, Mr. Bush wished the team well as practice resumed. Ryan and I were done with our portion of practice, so we took the opportunity to talk a bit longer with Mr. Bush. After all, it's not every day that one gets the opportunity to rub shoulders with a future president. Mr. Bush was very easy to talk to. He asked us a few questions and got the conversation underway. As we were talking, he actually noticed that we kept looking over to the sideline of the practice field where our wives were standing and asked us if they wanted to come over. That was great! As Sarah and Bethany were walking over, I realized that Sarah had snagged one of our practice footballs to have autographed, so I snuck out for a brief moment to do the same. We talked for about 15 minutes or so before he had to leave for a few more campaign obligations he was attending later that evening.

Then in Tampa in 2006, we heard that President Bush was in town, campaigning for his brother, Jeb Bush, who was the governor of the state of Florida and up for reelection in a few weeks. We also heard that the president was going to try to make it out to a practice and meet with the team. He is a huge sports fan; his family actually owned the Texas Rangers Major League Baseball team at one point, and President Bush has not lost his passion for sports. I hear that when he can, he makes time to meet different professional teams in the cities he visits.

The 2006 meeting in Tampa Bay felt like déjà vu. He arrived at our facilities with the men in black leading the way for his entourage (which was even larger this time) and even more media personnel. This time I noticed armed guards in his entourage, including two marksmen on the roof of our facility overlooking our practice fields and the surrounding areas. These two men were equipped with two of the biggest and scariest-looking rifles I have ever seen. I was mindful not to make any sudden or quick movements in the president's direction, just to be safe! Coach Gruden and the captains of the team led him to where the rest of us had formed a semicircle to greet him. His presentation to us was much the same as in Green Bay, only this time, he spent more time emphasizing the influence we have on kids in this country, and he encouraged us all to take extra effort to give back to those kids by being great examples they can look up to. And this time, he spent a lot of time talking to all of us individually. He was especially excited to connect with those players who were from the state of Texas.

The NFL has provided me with many wonderful opportunities, and these two experiences rank near the top. After President Bush left our practice field, the players mentioned that regardless of whether they voted for him or even liked him, they enjoyed meeting him that day.

Thanks to my status as an NFL player, I was presented with the opportunity to be the keynote speaker at a prayer breakfast on a U.S. military base in Mannheim, Germany. The organization that invited me is called Unlimited Potential, Inc. and is actually a ministry that uses baseball to communicate the gospel. Tom Roy, the founder of UPI, is a good friend of the Packers' chaplain, who suggested to Tom that I might be interested in going on a trip for UPI. I am as patriotic a person as you will ever meet, and when I was asked if I wanted to go to Germany to speak to and encourage our servicemen and women, I said yes right away.

This trip happened to be especially significant to me because we were in Germany during the first few days of the war in Iraq. We sensed a lot of tension and uncertainty on the base because the war was underway and many of these soldiers would soon be deployed. I spent a few days on the base to mingle with the troops and their families and to share a bit of my life with the troops at a prayer breakfast at the end of the week. I was surprised by the troops' response when I told them how proud I was of all of them and how thankful to them I was for defending our freedom. I was kind of nervous that I would come across as sounding a little cheesy, but after telling them my appreciation, everyone accepted it gratefully.

I have had other opportunities to talk to troops and veterans, and I am never quite prepared for their displays of passion and gratitude when I give them my sincere appreciation for their service. On one such occasion I had the opportunity to meet about ten of our Iraq War veterans at a space shuttle launch at Cape Canaveral. On this night, NASA community relations brought in ten heroes who had been severely wounded in Iraq and who were being cared for in our local veterans' hospital in Tampa. I sat and talked with each one of them individually throughout the evening, hearing their stories about what happened and how they were recovering. These men were missing eyes, arms, legs, and portions of their skulls, but they knew their fighting made a difference in all of our lives back here in the States. It was one of the most emotional experiences I have ever been a part of.

I have never felt more proud to be an American than I did that night. The men and women I spoke with will have difficulties for the rest of their lives; some will be completely dependent on others to do menial tasks like eating and drinking, but none of them are allowing bitterness to ruin their lives. In fact, they accept the heroes' welcome they so deserve wherever they go. The launch was canceled that night because of the weather, but our guests of honor were the hit of the show. I know I can speak for all who were there that we were all made to be better Americans after having had the chance to meet these amazing young men and women who have given so much of themselves so we can all live freely in the greatest country in the world.

MORE TRUE HEROES

Many fans never hear about the amazing ways many NFL players are investing in the lives of others. Players all over the league do many great things for deserving people, whether it be something big like providing a free, furnished home to a single mother as Warrick Dunn of the Atlanta Falcons does through his foundation every year, or smaller acts of service like spending time with injured war veterans or visiting schools to encourage children to keep working hard so they can reach their dreams. I am not trying to prove the worth of NFL players, but it is nice to see that so many of us in the NFL are not selfishly squandering our platform and opportunity to help others. It is important to many of us to use our influence to inspire others and improve their lives. I involve myself in the lives of young cancer patients and survivors wherever I can. I continue to show my respect for our servicemen and women and have had many small opportunities to meet them in various parts of the world and to show them our appreciation and give them encouragement. These are just a few ways I have been blessed to give back and to bring joy and make a difference in others' lives. Many other players are doing all of that and more themselves.

Some of the NFL players' public service is well-publicized each year. However, many other things are going on behind the scenes. One player (who asked to remain anonymous) who spent only one season with us in Green Bay did something that no one even knew about until he was already gone. This player had grown up in hard times. He was an orphan and lived in various foster homes. His was a rough childhood of abuse, neglect, and fending for himself. He never knew the joy of the holidays and the excitement of waking up on Christmas morning to a tree surrounded by presents waiting to be opened. As he states, this was one of his greatest regrets.

As a result, this player is passionate about providing needy, troubled children with the wonderful Christmas experience he never had. This particular Christmas season, with the help of a member of the Packers' community-relations staff, he anonymously and secretively acquired a list of every single child in any hospital in the Green Bay area two days before Christmas. Each child was asked to name one gift he or she dreamed of receiving that Christmas. The children were told to write down any gift, regardless of how great or small. This player then purchased *every single gift* on those lists and had them wrapped and delivered for each child to open on Christmas morning. I was not aware that this had ever happened. No one in the media caught wind of it. Even the community-relations person who helped kept the secret until a year later.

Players are giving back to their communities and striving to better the lives of those around them in many other ways. The media gives a lot of attention to the negative side of players' activities and the mistakes they make each year, but much good activity is going on as well. I love to hear about the great ways players work to bless the lives of others, great or small, because that not only blesses those lives directly but also inspires those who hear about it to do the same for others. Many players are working hard in various charities, and that is the way it is supposed to be. Most of these players use their time and talents to benefit others and not to glorify themselves. Every year I seem to hear about a new and amazing way that a player has done something special for someone else, and that makes me very proud and even more motivated to do the same.

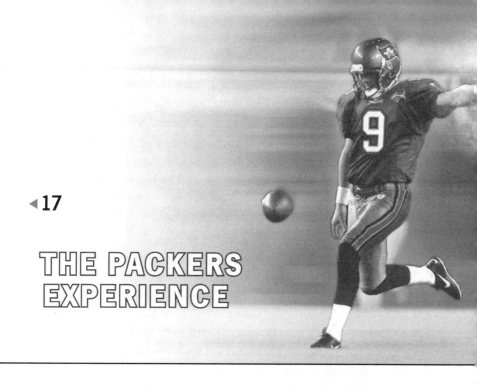

17

THE PACKERS EXPERIENCE

Being a member of the Green Bay Packers, possibly the most popular American sports franchise of all time, was an amazing experience. Whether we were on the road or at home, Packers fans were always there to offer their rowdy support. In a handful of road games, we had more fans in the stands than the home team did. That was the case in Arizona when we played the Cardinals. One time, when the Cardinals' offense was in a third and long situation, our fans were so loud that their offense had to call a time-out because they couldn't hear each other call the play. I haven't seen anything like that since. Anywhere in the country we traveled, we saw many green and gold shirts, hats, and jackets in and around our team hotel. Now that I am with the Tampa Bay Buccaneers, we see fans come to our hotels on the road, but not as many supporters as the Packers see.

PLAYING AT HOME

Packers home games are amazing experiences. It is hard to explain just how small Green Bay is, especially near the stadium. There is no huge metropolis. In fact, a small stretch of road with a few stores and a mall constitutes most of the city of Green Bay. Game day is the most unique NFL experience anyone could ever experience. The stadium sits between a few small businesses and residences. Homes are located just outside the parking lot and right across the street. (I imagine those home values are appreciating well!) The setting is unlike any other professional stadium I have ever seen and certainly provides a unique professional sports experience.

People from all over the state line the surrounding streets, making the whole area look like a fair. For me as a player, the experience was awesome. On game days, Bethany drove me to the stadium down one of the back streets. The closer we got to the stadium, the more like a fair the scene became. Residents encouraged motorists to park in their lawns (for a "small" fee), tailgaters were everywhere, kids played catch in the street, grown-ups played catch in the street, and a myriad of other people just wandered around, mingling. Many people set up booths and sold food, hats, drinks, and the most popular food in Wisconsin—beer-battered bratwursts.

After navigating through the masses, we made our way toward our players' parking lot, which was secured by a large fence and security gate. Driving to our parking lot, we felt like movie stars walking the red carpet at a huge event. We drove slowly past rows and rows of people lined up on both sides of the driveway who were screaming at the top of their lungs in support for that game. Most of these people showed up five or six hours before games to start their tailgating ritual. These are the most supportive and passionate fans in the NFL by far. Great season or bad, win or lose, every game at Lambeau Field will sell out, and the carnival atmosphere outside the stadium will be as rowdy and packed as ever.

Everyday life in Green Bay, for a Packers player, was a lot of fun. Because of the huge, passionate following the team enjoys and the small-town feel of the Green Bay area, players couldn't go anywhere without being recognized. You didn't have to be Brett Favre for the fans to be excited to see you; you just had to be a player. Bethany and I often walked around the local mall because the weather was too cold for us to do much else. We didn't get involved in hunting, ice fishing, or anything else of that nature that many locals enjoyed doing in the winter months, so we watched a lot of movies, hung out at the small mall down the road from the stadium, grabbed a bite to eat at a few different restaurants, or just visited some friends during our time off. I felt a little weird walking through town and seeing people staring. I certainly wasn't a well-known player, but the fans made me feel as if I were. I was flattered to have someone come up to me just to say hi and tell me what a huge fan he or she was. Wherever I went, I could rest assured I would meet avid Packers fans and hear stories of their special connection to the NFL's most popular team.

GREAT PLAYERS, GREAT PEOPLE

Whenever people ask me about my time as a Green Bay Packer, they want to know what Brett Favre is like. Contrary to popular belief, Brett Favre is actually human! He is a normal guy just like the rest of us—except, of course, that he is a record-holding, Super Bowl winning, future NFL hall of famer. Aside from that, he is no different from the rest of us. Playing with Brett was a great thrill for me. He is one of the best quarterbacks in NFL history, and even before I met him, I was a huge fan of his. He has always been one of the most entertaining quarterbacks to watch because of his ability to make throws most other QBs cannot make and because of his flair for dramatics, making risky throws that worked because of his incredible arm strength. I often saw Brett make throws and wondered how he was able to do it. In practice, he threw deep balls to receivers that looked like punts.

One "Brett Favre moment" came in a game at home against the Minnesota Vikings. Brett dropped back to pass, but the play quickly fell apart. The next moment Brett was racing to his right as fast as he could with two or three defenders gaining on him from behind. Most other QBs would have just thrown the ball out of bounds and been content to live another day. But just before Brett reached the sideline, he fired the ball underhand to Aman Green for a touchdown. Those of us who have played football before know how hard it is to throw a ball accurately or with any strength underhanded, not to mention that Brett was running full speed to his right and was about to get clobbered by a couple 280-plus pound defenders. It all happened pretty fast, but it was one of the coolest plays I had the privilege of seeing in person.

The characteristic of Brett Favre that I respect the most is his professionalism. He never yells at a player who does something wrong, but he will show frustration when he messes up himself. Often a quarterback will be visibly upset with a receiver who drops a pass—and in the heat of the moment, it can be hard not to—but Brett never does. He may talk to him respectfully on the sideline, but he will never show up a player on the field during a game. I greatly respect that. Brett realizes that all his teammates play with 100-percent effort and will make mistakes from time to time, just as he will. As a teammate of his, I can tell you that his professionalism was his biggest leadership attribute. The team knew they could count on Brett to always give his all and be supportive at all times, and that made us all want to play just as hard. I know Brett's on-the-field leadership is a huge reason he has been one of the best players in the NFL for so long and has been on some of the best teams in the NFL.

I was surprised at how "normal" the players were when I first entered the NFL. For some reason, we as fans make professional athletes and many other celebrities seem as though they are not like everyone else. But the only difference between them and everyone else is what they do. In Brett's case, he is as normal as any of my friends back home—except for his obvious professional accomplishments. He loves to golf and hunt and is an incredibly generous person. He gives his time and efforts to those in need. He has an amazing wife, Deanna, and two beautiful daughters. He is a family man just like many of us and has a life outside of football. Only his fame makes his day-to-day life different from the normal person's. He is not able to go to shopping malls or watch a movie at the theater without sneaking in the back door after the room is dark and leaving just before the movie ends. That part of his life is certainly different from the average person's. I am a bigger fan of Brett's now that I have gotten to know him and watch him play in person, and I have a great deal of respect for what he has accomplished, both as a football player and as a man.

FREE AGENCY

A lot of people who follow professional sports will hear about players every year who are free agents. Free agency just means that a player is no longer contractually bound to his former team and is free to sign with whomever he chooses. The 2003 season was the last year on my Green Bay contract. That meant I was a free agent after that season and could sign with any team that wanted me. This was my first experience with free agency, and honestly, it was not a fun experience. Unless a lot of teams want you and are willing to offer huge contracts, it can be extremely stressful.

My last year with the Packers was not a record-breaking year, but I had solid numbers and was an accountable, dependable performer on the team. I had already proven that I could play at a high level, having recorded the second-highest net punting average in team history. I also broke David Beverly's 23-year-old Packers record for most consecutive punts without a block (274, set from 1977 to 1980) by extending my own streak of unblocked punts to 308. That last record is somewhat ironic because my special-teams coach a few years earlier made such a huge deal that I was too slow. I was not the best punter the team had ever had, but I was confident that I did not fall far behind the best punters in team history. However, after all my experiences with the team, the community, and the Packers' faithful fans, I felt as though my time there was at its end.

Free agency is like open season. I could seek out other teams' interests in me, and I could sense the direction my former team seemed to be heading with the punting position. As my agent and I negotiated with the Green Bay front office, I realized they did not intend for me to be their punter for the future. My agent and the Packers' general manager and/or salary-cap manager handled the negotiations. I asked my agent not to tell me everything the team said in their negotiations. I knew they would say a lot of negative things about my abilities in order to make us feel less confident about our worth to other teams. That would have led us to sign whatever contract they offered, good or bad. As the negotiations continued, the conversation between my agent and their salary-cap negotiator became pretty ugly. I knew I needed to see what team out there really wanted to sign me to their squad, and that was exactly what I did.

Teams who are looking at a new player will fly that player to their facility to talk with the coaches and visit the team's complex. It is sort of a two-way interview. They want to get to know the player a little better, and the player wants to interact with the coaches as well as see what type of facilities the teams have to offer. I took a quick trip to the Miami Dolphins, who just happened to be my favorite NFL team when I was a kid, and it went pretty well. They seemed fairly interested, but they were at odds with their old punter, whose contract had just expired as mine had. My feeling was that they wanted him back, but they just did not want to pay him the amount he and his agent were looking for. It was not the best situation for me because I had to wait and see how things played out between them before I would know if they were really interested in me.

After that visit, I flew directly to Tampa to do the same type of visit, but this visit went quite a bit differently. The team made it pretty clear that they wanted to sign me right away and did not want to look at any other free-agent punters that off season. The special-teams coach, Rich Bisaccia, said he watched a lot of my film from the previous years and drew up a chart on most of my punts, and that led him to believe I was one of the best of the free-agent punters that were available that year. It was nice to think about starting from scratch someplace new and playing for a team that showed that they genuinely wanted me there. That was not the case with the Packers. When the Packers offered me only the same contract Tampa Bay offered, they made my decision for me. I was heading south to play in Florida, where there was no state income tax, the weather was much better, and the team was excited to have me playing there.

It's funny how things work out though. As I look back, I was pretty nervous about leaving Green Bay. They were the only team I had played for. Ryan and Sarah were still there, as well as a few other close friends I had on the team, and Bethany and I were pretty settled in the area. The decision to leave was difficult; in fact, I was leaning toward going back if Green Bay would pay me just a little bit more than Tampa was offering to offset the obvious advantages that punting in Florida has over punting in the frigid Midwest.

Playing in the warm Florida weather for the entire season and not having to kick a flat, frozen ball in some of the NFL's windiest conditions, my punting average was sure to improve, and that would translate into me having more of an opportunity to extend my career. When the Packers' financial person laughed at my contract request, I told my agent that the negotiations between us and Green Bay were over and that I would accept Tampa Bay's contract offer.

That's when all my reservations and the nervousness I had about leaving Green Bay quickly turned into excitement about the new experiences Bethany and I were about to have.

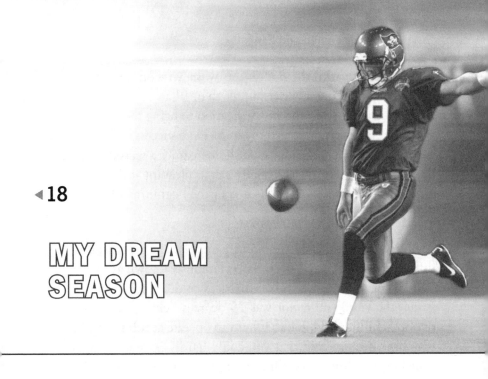

18

MY DREAM SEASON

The Tampa Bay Buccaneers were not offering me a huge contract, but they made it very clear to me that they thought that I had the potential to be a great addition to their team and could be their punter for a very long time. I signed a three-year contract. I was convinced that my move to this new team, who believed in me and who enjoyed an excellent weather environment, would be a great career move for me. As it turned out, it was the best career move I could have made.

Moving to a new team in a new city was like switching to a new school. It was very exciting, but Bethany and I really did not know what to expect. We loved the city right away, and the weather, the palm trees, and the beautiful beaches made us very comfortable right from the start. That was what I was hoping for when I signed there. I wanted an opportunity to improve my skills and become one of the best.

My first season went very well. It was clear from the start that my decision to sign with the Buccaneers was a wise one and that I was on my way to being a better punter than I had ever been. In addition to my work ethic and my dedication to being the best I can be, two other factors encouraged my immediate success in Tampa. The first is the weather. We play eight home games a season in Tampa, Florida, and the weather is usually just as pleasant at the end of the regular season in December as it is in the beginning of the season in September.

Kicking a great punt during home games late in the season is very difficult in Green Bay. Green Bay is famously known as the Frozen Tundra for the obvious reason that it is cold! At our coldest home game, the windchill factor was 25 degrees below zero. That type of bone-chilling cold makes it hard to operate at full strength. You may have been so cold that you could hardly open a bottle or use your fingers. Think of battling through that in the middle of a football game. Playing in those conditions is possible, and Green Bay is not a bad place or the toughest place to play. But playing well in such extreme conditions is difficult, and there is an advantage to playing for a team that has significantly better weather.

Green Bay is not only cold, it is incredibly windy. I'm always surprised when people ask me if wind is really a significant factor in punting. A serious headwind or crosswind makes punting a strong ball with a great spiral very difficult. Without a spiral, a punt will not travel far at all on windy days. Picture yourself when you were a kid, and imagine kicking a fully pumped-up soccer ball. Now imagine kicking a half-filled soccer ball. I think you'll agree that the pumped-up ball will go much further. Now imagine kicking into a 25 mile-per-hour wind. The pumped-up ball will still go farther than the flat one, but it will not go nearly as far as a pumped-up ball kicked in windless conditions. In Lambeau Field late in the winter, I kicked footballs that were cold, flat, and rock hard, and I did it in a steady 20-plus mile-per-hour wind. The balls I had to kick in those conditions did not even come close to those in late December in Tampa, where the temperature is in the mid seventies to mid eighties. My average in Green Bay would steadily go down late in the year, whereas my average in Tampa would stay the same or even improve because the conditions are absolutely ideal throughout the entire season. At the punting and kicking position, the ball makes all the difference. A great ball in perfect conditions gives the kicker a huge advantage over someone kicking in adverse conditions much of the year.

The other major factor in my success in Tampa is the coaching staff. From day one it was evident to me that the coaching staff at Tampa made the effort to get to know each player personally and use encouragement as well as demand to get the most out of each player. Some NFL coaches think they have to relate to their players through intimidation and fear. We players are all very aware of the fact that if we do not play well, we could get fired. Plenty of other players are out there who want our jobs, and we don't need to be reminded of that fact on a daily basis as a form of motivation. This business has no room for players to become complacent and not work hard to help their team win games, and if they do, they should lose their jobs. But if fear and intimidation are used too much, they can wear on the players and zap the motivation out of them.

That was not the case in Tampa at all. I have been challenged, pushed, and driven by the coaching staff, but always in a way that added to my internal drive to be the best I can be, not just for myself but for the coaches and the rest of the team as well. My best guess is that few coaching staffs in the NFL operate in a way that makes their players want to win for them as much as they want to win for themselves. From day one, Coach Gruden, Rich Bisaccia, and the rest of the Tampa Bay coaching staff made me a better player by making me feel like we were all in this together.

That first season in Tampa was the best of my career to that point, and I knew I had all the pieces put together to improve myself to be one of the best in the league, which is my drive each and every season.

My season average was exactly the same as my best season average in Green Bay, but my net punting average was better than it had ever been. My numbers for the entire season were actually much higher than I had ever had until my last three games that season. As Coach Bisaccia always tells me, I dominated all but three games that season.

The third to last game we played was a home game against the New Orleans Saints in an absolute windstorm. I punted about six times, and every single punt was into that difficult wind. The Saints' punter struggled to kick the ball far as well. My average for the day was in the low thirties, which brought my season average down quite a bit.

The next two games were against the Carolina Panthers and the Arizona Cardinals. Both of those games were in good conditions, but I think I lost my focus a bit after the disastrous game against the Saints. I had been staring a record-breaking season in the face and was on track to crush my personal-best season statistics, but my numbers went down quite a bit after that one game, and that took a lot away from the tremendous season I was having.

I didn't quit trying hard; my effort was there for the final two games. But I actually tried a bit too hard to make up for the hit my stats had taken. Trying too hard can be just as destructive as not trying hard enough. I was inconsistent in those last two games, and my numbers were mediocre at best. I finished the season very well considering what I had done in previous seasons, and was once again a Pro Bowl alternate. But I knew deep inside that I let three games slip out of my hands, and I learned a valuable lesson about keeping focus all the way to the end.

Coming so close to the Pro Bowl but not quite getting voted in that season left a bad taste in my mouth that entire off-season. I have always wanted to win a Super Bowl, but that's not something a punter has a lot of control over. I would have to play well and be on the right team at the right time to make that happen, and I hope it does before my NFL career is over. However, my number one personal goal was to make it to a Pro Bowl, and after coming so close in the 2004 season, I was more motivated than ever as I looked forward to the 2005 season. My off-season workout was much the same as it had always been. After every season, I look back at what I did well and not so well, and I work hard to improve. That was exactly what I did because I knew then that I was a Pro Bowl–caliber punter.

The 2005 season came, and right from the start I could see that my hard work in the off-season was paying off. Through our four preseason games I led the NFL with an average of more than 53 yards per punt, and the groove I was in carried me into the regular season. Week after week, I punted great, which not only helped me get closer to my personal goal but also played a huge role in us winning games and making the playoffs that year.

A lot goes into having a great punting average besides just kicking the ball as far as possible. During the course of a game I will be asked to punt from various places on the field. If our offense is not doing very well, I will have a better opportunity to have a higher punting average simply because I am required to kick the ball farther each time. However, if our offense is doing pretty well but gets stopped just outside of field-goal range, I need to punt the ball shorter in order to pin the other team inside their own 20-yard line and ideally inside the 10. If I am punting from the 40-yard line and I hit a great punt to the 10-yard line, we win on that play. However, that means I only had a 30-yard punt even though it was a great play for us. If I am having to do that a lot in the course of a game, my average will be very low and won't reflect just how good a game I might have had.

In my 2005 season, I had a good mixture of full-field, long punts and the short "pooch" punts I just described. That played a big role in me having an even better season than I had the previous year. Week in and week out, I was coming out of games with great averages, and I was leading the NFC in average yards per punt. As the season was nearing the end, I realized I was probably the front-runner to go the Pro Bowl that year. Unlike all of the other positions, the Pro Bowl only takes one punter and one kicker per conference each year. You have to finish number one to get your shot.

The last few games made me pretty nervous. I was competing against one other punter, who was having a great year as well, and I could only hope that I continued to punt well and get plenty of opportunities to punt in full-field situations. In each of the last few weeks, I was relieved to see I was edging out the other punter and keeping my lead atop the NFC.

The process of being selected to the Pro Bowl is threefold. The first part is the fan vote. Fans can cast their votes a few different ways, but the main way is to vote online at NFL.com. The fan vote counts as one-third of the voting.

The second part of voting is the players' vote. Each team is given ballots so players can vote on every position. Players are not allowed to vote for themselves or any of their own teammates. Also, because we are an NFC team, we are only allowed to vote for NFC players.

The third and final part of the voting is the coaches' ballot. The coaches are under the same voting rules as the players. They are not allowed to vote for any players on their own team, and they can only vote for players in their conference.

Fan voting closed just before the players and coaches all voted, and I found out I had the majority of the fan vote for the season. That was exciting to hear, but it made me nervous too because I knew that was only one-third of the whole voting process, and I was going to need more than just the fan vote. Two weeks before the last game of the season, I still had the number one NFC average. We all cast our ballots as a team, and then we had to wait until the next Wednesday's practice to find out who had made it as a starter or an alternate, which I had been twice before. I didn't want to get my hopes up because I felt like I deserved to go, and not being selected would have been hard to handle.

Wednesday morning finally arrived, and I was, understandably, a little anxious to hear the results of the voting. None of the coaches or media personnel were talking. I wasn't sure if they had gotten the news yet, and I wondered if I was going to have to wait until later that afternoon. Fortunately, I didn't have to wait until the end of the day to hear the news. After the morning walk-through, Coach called the team into a team huddle to make a few announcements, including the results of the Pro Bowl selections. A couple members of the team were selected as alternates, which is a great honor, and two of my teammates made it as starters. Ronde Barber, one of our star cornerbacks, and his twin brother, the star running back for the New York Giants, were both selected. Our star linebacker Derrick Brooks was selected to play in his ninth-straight Pro Bowl game. After Coach Gruden took his sweet time to mention every other player who was an alternate and the other two starters, he finally said the words I had waited my entire career to hear. "This last guy has had the best year of any Buccaneer punter in history and really deserves this honor. Josh Bidwell has been selected to his first Pro Bowl! Congratulations, Josh!"

This was the icing on the cake for what had already been a very special year. Bethany and I had found out in April that she was pregnant with our first child and was due around the end of December. My doctors had told us at the beginning of my cancer that I might not be able to have kids. But many other men had survived the same cancer and were able to have children, so Bethany and I simply trusted that God would either provide us with a child naturally or would lead us to adopt. Either way, Bethany and I were excited to be parents.

We were so thankful when we found out she was pregnant. I know many couples suffer heartache as they wait and wait for a child. Bethany and I had a long wait as well, which made us really rely on God and trust that His plan in this area of our lives was perfect. Couples do a lot of soul-searching when they are battling through the slow process of becoming pregnant. It is not a sure thing for everyone, and often, only time will tell whether they will be able to have children. Time passed for us, and we started to wonder too.

I will always remember the look in Bethany's eyes when she gave me the news. I could see her joy and her overwhelming love and happiness for me because she knew how much I wanted to have children. As I looked back on the first few weeks after being diagnosed with cancer, remembering how the news coming in kept getting worse and worse, I was amazed to see how God had turned the tables. Now, the news in our lives was getting better and better.

So the 2005 season had started out with the amazing news of Bethany's pregnancy, and it ended with my first selection to the Pro Bowl. Bethany and I were completely overwhelmed. We found out about the Pro Bowl on the third-to-last Wednesday of the season. One week later, our beautiful baby boy, Brady John Bidwell, was born! Brady came on the Wednesday before a home game against the New Orleans Saints. Concentrating on the sideline that Sunday was hard for me, knowing that my beautiful wife was home watching with our brand-new baby.

Bethany arranged to have a special message put up on the replay screen on the scoreboard during the second half of that game. It read, "Congratulations, Josh, on becoming a dad and making the Pro Bowl! We love you, Bethany and Brady." My eyes filled with tears, and my ears were filled with the roar of the crowd's huge ovation.

Our regular season ended with us making the playoffs. In the first round, we had a home game against the Washington Redskins. We played great but fell short by just a few points, and so my dream season came to an end. I guess the only way the season could have gone any better would have been if we had been able to go on to win the Super Bowl. To have so much to look forward to as the season began and to get even more by the end of the year made this one of the best years of my life. As Bethany and I look back on 2005, we can do nothing but thank God for giving us such a memorable year.

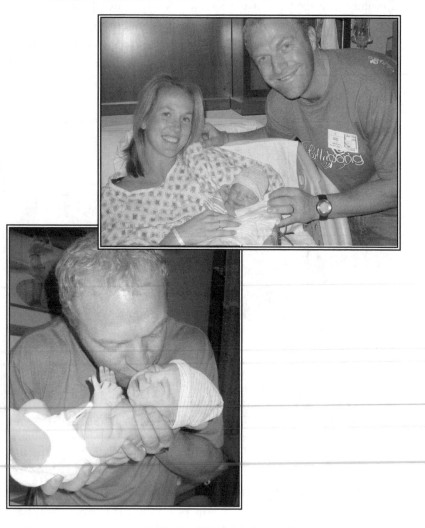

19

THE 2006 NFL PRO BOWL

All I knew about the NFL Pro Bowl, I had learned from watching the game each year on television. The Pro Bowl is the NFL's version of an all-star game. The best of the best in the NFL for that season are voted in and get to spend a week in Hawaii together with their families. I was always impressed with the players who were voted in each year, and I honestly never imagined being voted in myself. It was a real goal of mine, but I also had a realistic view of just how hard it is to make it. It was a great thrill to have been given that prize for the hard work I had put in to becoming the best I can be.

After I was voted in, I received a packet explaining how the whole process would work. I found out that my family and I would be flown out to Hawaii a week before the game. The NFL gave each player either two free first-class tickets to Hawaii or four free coach-class tickets. Bethany and I took the four free tickets because we wanted her parents and my dad to experience the whole week with us. We were given rooms at the JW Marriott Ihilani Resort and Spa at Ko Olina. It is the most amazing resort I have ever been to, with a huge pool, beautiful outdoor dining, and its own private beach. Right next to the hotel was a huge field, which is converted every year into a full-length football field. It was temporarily fenced off for our practices during the week. The NFL skills challenge is held at this same place each year, pitting the league's best athletes against each other in different challenges to find out who is the strongest, the fastest, the best catcher, and the best passer. The field-goal kickers even have a small challenge.

The hotel was completely closed to the public for that week except for a special list of players, coaches, and their families. Each player receives one room and a discount on any additional rooms for family members. Having Bethany's parents and my dad there with us was a treat. The Pro Bowl is a once in a lifetime experience, and our parents never get the chance to rub shoulders with NFL players the way Bethany and I do every year. The experience was particularly meaningful for my dad because he and I have always been huge football fans. We watched NFL games together as I was growing up, and now he was able to go to the Pro Bowl for the entire week and hang out with the best players in the league at one of the most beautiful places on earth. I can't describe the joy I felt as I watched him having the time of his life and as I saw how proud he was of me. He still drives me to be the best person I can be in all areas of my life, and I know that he was honored to be a part of something that was so special and that I had worked so hard to attain.

To top it all off, our brand-new baby boy, Brady John, was with us, and we were able to get a lot of pictures with him to commemorate the event and to reflect on the incredible year we had enjoyed. When my dad arrived at the resort, he met Brady for the first time. Brady was born in Florida, and my dad was not able to fly out to be with us. I will never forget the first time he saw his little grandson.

He didn't stop smiling the whole time. Dad and I spent a lot of time relaxing together at the resort, but one of my favorite moments was seeing him fall asleep with little Brady napping on his chest.

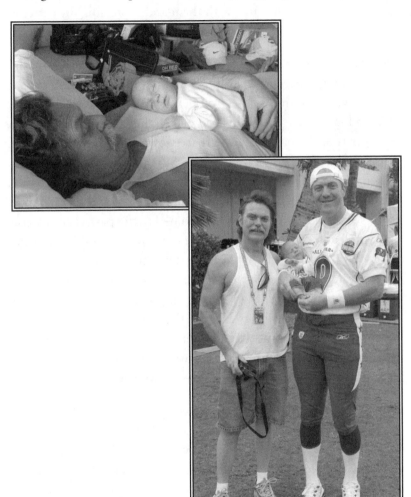

I mentioned that most of the players and families are flown out a week before the game, but I was invited to attend an extra event. A representative from the NFL called to ask if I would like to fly out a few days early to watch the Super Bowl on a Navy warship with some troops that had just gotten back from serving in the Persian Gulf. I could not have been more honored and excited to be a part of that experience. I am so proud of our servicemen and women, so spending some quality time with them and expressing my extreme gratitude and pride in them was an opportunity of a lifetime.

My father-in-law and I flew out early and were given a tour by the commanding officers of the ship. I had never been on any sort of military vessel, so this was an eye-opener. We were shown the entire ship and saw where the sailors had been living and working for the better part of the past year. The space was cramped to say the least. This vessel was not designed for comfort; it was a state-of-the-art war machine with some technology we weren't even allowed to see. We quickly noticed the tremendous amount of pride each sailor had in this ship. It was not only their home for the past year but also their protection against very real and dangerous enemies. After the tour, we finished the day by heading down to their mess hall to eat and to watch the Super Bowl together on a big-screen television that had been set up for us. Many of the officers brought their families aboard to hang out with us as well. The mood was great. We were all excited to spend time with each other, the families were thrilled to have their loved ones back, and we all had a fun time razzing each other as we rooted for the teams we wanted to win.

The entire week was absolutely amazing. We spent a lot of time relaxing by the pool or on the beach. The whole experience is designed to be a reward for the players and coaches who are there. The practices were only about 30 minutes long and did not require much from us physically. The team had to learn only a few plays for the game, so we didn't have to study film or attend as many meetings as we would have during the season. The coaches did a great job of not putting a lot of pressure on us and of allowing us to relax and enjoy the week.

Every player had free rein and could do pretty much what he

wanted. The NFL had connections set up all over the island so we could participate in such diverse activities as enjoying a private snorkeling adventure or flying on a refueling mission with some pilots on the nearby military base. However, Bethany and I had decided earlier that we did not want to spend the week trying to do it all, but rather relaxing and enjoying this dream experience with our families and new baby boy. As I look back, I'm so glad we did it that way. The week went by fast enough as it was, and we were able to enjoy every day to its fullest.

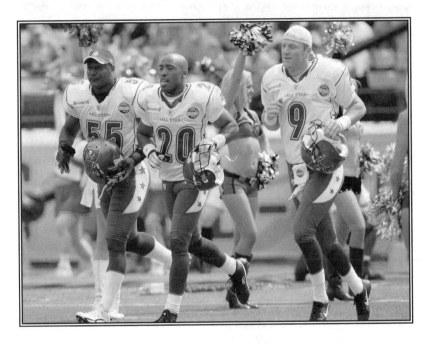

Game day was a unique experience. We arrived at Aloha Stadium with a capacity crowd welcoming us. We were all introduced with any teammates who were there. We had no real pressure to perform, aside from our personal desire to do well, and the fans supported both teams. Throughout the game, whoever made a great play was honored as if he were the hometown hero. The game was simply a fun way to cap off a great season.

One other aspect of my first Pro Bowl experience helped make the trip a memorable one. Believe it or not, I was not the only graduate from Douglas High School in Winston, Oregon, who was playing in this game. Troy Polamalu, one of the most talented and recognizable NFL players today, was playing on the opposing team. Troy and I grew up together just outside of Winston. Troy lived with his Aunt Shelly, his Uncle Salu, and his two cousins, Darren and Brandon, who were my age. I was good friends with his two cousins, and we played on the same teams growing up. Troy is about five years younger than me, so we were never able to play on the same team together, but he was always around, and he was as good as or better than we were even though he was so much younger. We could tell he was going to be a very special athlete. He was a star in basketball and baseball as well as a dominant force on the football field. Troy could have been very successful in base-ball had he chosen that route instead, but he chose to pursue his football career when he accepted a scholarship to the University of Southern California. There he became a two-time all-American as a free safety.

Today, many fans know Troy by his nicknames: the Tazmanian Devil, the Flying Hawaiian, and the Samoan Headhunter. He has long, black hair that hangs out of his helmet and nearly covers the entire number on the back of his jersey. As I stood on the field opposite his team as the national anthem was being played, I could not help but look over and marvel at the fact that two boys from Douglas High School were about to play against each other in the NFL Pro Bowl. And even more amazing to me was seeing Troy standing there as one of the best and most recognizable players in the NFL. I take a lot of pride in representing our small community as I continue my career in the NFL, and I know Troy feels the same way. Standing on that sideline, I enjoyed one of the proudest moments of my career.

20

LOOKING BACK TO SEE MY FUTURE

I can now see that everything I have experienced has helped to make me into the man I am today. Even as I finish writing this book in my home in Oregon, my wife and I have just had our second baby boy, Aaron Robert Bidwell. He was born just a couple of days ago and is yet another living reminder of how incredibly blessed I am. God's blessing on my life goes far beyond my career and how the world views me. He is working in me internally as much as He is blessing me externally. He truly has captured my heart and given me the strength to overcome anything He allows to come my way.

The wisdom I have now enables me to see just how far from God I allowed myself to go as a child. My self-worth was wrapped up in my performance. As long as I was well-behaved off the field and successful on the field, I felt as though I mattered and was important to other people. I endured many ups and downs as I struggled to impress others, and that made accepting God's grace and forgiveness extremely difficult. In the world's eyes, the formula for success is based on our own efforts and earning everything ourselves.

In my early years, like most people I talk to, I thought being a Christian was being good or doing religious things. I thought this would please God, and He would accept me and give me heaven as a reward for my good and sincere efforts. When I realized that I had underestimated God (who is holy, righteous, and just) and overestimated my own goodness and efforts, the gospel made sense to me for the first time. I saw that Jesus is God, that He lived a sinless life as a man and died on my behalf, paying the penalty for my sin. I realized I needed to believe this to be true, accept this payment as my own, and place my faith in the reality of God's Son and His work on the cross. I gladly exchanged my sin for His salvation; I quit trying to earn my way into God's good graces and accepted the free grace of His forgiveness. I became a Christian, a son of God, adopted into His stable and eternal family.

You can undoubtedly look back over your life and see God's work in your past as well. He does all He can to draw us into a relationship with Him, stopping short of forcing us against our will. If we will reflect on our past, we will see evidence of His work in our lives. This is His way of saying, "I have always been here with you, and I want you to be in my family. I want you to accept the gift of forgiveness and eternal life. I want you to place your faith in Me—not in your good works, not in your religious activities, but in the person and the work of Jesus." This decision changed my life. It gave me assurance that my life had meaning, that my death would not separate me from God but would fully unite me with Him. It also changed the way I related to God and others. Life was no longer all about me; I was learning to live as Jesus did, in obedience to God.

Unlike Jesus, I am not perfect in this endeavor, but I see God's hand changing my life, and I love what I see. Having read this far in this book, it would be a shame if you missed this point. God loves you and desires for you to place your faith in Him and in the work of His Son. He wants to establish an eternal relationship with you. If you believe you are not able to live according to God's perfect standard, if you believe you are unable to save yourself from the consequences of your sin through religious works, if you believe that Jesus is who He said He is and died to pay for your sin, all that's left to do is for you to place your faith in Him and nothing else. This decision is confirmed by your intellect and enjoyed emotionally, but it is primarily a choice of your will. You could express to God your heart and will right now in prayer. Talk to Him about your sin, repent (turn) from that sin and from self-righteousness, and simply accept His forgiveness and thank Him for His kindness and grace. Tell Him you desire to walk with Him and obey Him. God knows what's going on inside you, and He will be glad to hear from you. Today, right now, would be a great time to tell Him how you feel.

What evidence has God left in your life? God has been working in your life to get your attention. He wants to bring you into a relationship with Him, and He wants to make you into a new person—the person He wants you to be. Take a few moments and look back at the events that have brought you to this point in your life. Where has God been working? What has He been trying to do in and through you? Who are some of the people you have met who have shown you glimpses of God? What about those hard times in your life that you had no idea how you would ever get through? Consider the ways God has been working in your life and ask yourself the most important question you can ever ask: Do you know God personally?

Maybe you have given your life to Jesus before but that was so long ago and your life seems so far from Him that you aren't sure whether your decision was real. Or perhaps you are positive that you have never made the decision to give your life to Jesus Christ. That can all change this very moment. You can know for sure, without a doubt, that you will spend eternity in heaven with God if you sincerely pray this simple prayer. It is not the prayer that gets you to heaven; it is believing in your heart every word of the prayer. If that is what you want to do now, if you want to know that you will be in heaven with God when you die, simply pray this prayer and mean it with all your heart:

> *Lord Jesus, I need You. Thank You for dying on the cross for my sins. I open the door of my life and receive You as my Savior and Lord. Thank You for forgiving my sins and giving me eternal life. Take control of the throne of my life. Make me the kind of person You want me to be.*

If you prayed this prayer and meant it with all your heart, your new faith in Jesus Christ has cleared you of all your sins. Today and forever you can be sure that you will spend eternity in heaven with God when you die. It is very important that you tell another Christian—perhaps a friend or someone at a church—that you made this decision so he or she can help you walk and grow in your new relationship with God. God has a great plan for your life. Seek Him with all your heart, and you'll be amazed at the wonders He will do in your heart and in your life.

I gave my life to Jesus when I was in high school, and He is continuing to work in me, patiently molding me into the man He wants me to be and equipping me to handle all that comes my way for His glory and His honor. Jesus said to "let your light shine before men, that they may see your good deeds and praise your Father in heaven" (Matthew 5:16). I benefited from others shining God's light in their lives as I pondered a relationship with God, and now, as I continue to walk in God's plan for my life, I have resolved to use the knowledge of His work in my past to strengthen and encourage me to walk with Him daily.

During the worst part of my year battling cancer, I did just that. I remember lying in bed late one night, hurting from the surgery that left a large incision down the length of my stomach, sick and weak from the chemotherapy treatments, and a bit discouraged at the frail physical state I was in. I began to look back on the events of my life that led me to that point. As I lay there pondering my past, I soon saw the evidence of all that God had done to prepare me to handle my battle with cancer. He had been teaching me many small lessons to equip me for this battle, which He knew I would eventually face. I did not realize that while I was going through such tough times and learning other lessons as a child, God was teaching me more than just what I learned at the time. He was building in me the ability to rely on Him in any and every situation, to prove His faithfulness and love in my life, knowing I would need to rely on those lessons as I battled cancer later on in my life. That was exactly what I rested on as my life hung in the balance.

At every stage of my life thus far, I have had a lot of time to reflect on my spiritual journey and the events that ultimately led me to commit my life to the Lord. We often tend to focus on the bad in our lives, especially when we are in the midst of them, and say to God, *Why me?* God tells us very clearly in His Word that He is constantly pursuing us to have a relationship with us, and He desires nothing but the best for us. I was sad when my parents got divorced, I missed having my sister around as I grew up, I was afraid to move to a new town with a new family, and I tried to understand where God was as all of this turmoil was unfolding. The old adage "hindsight is 20/20" really is true. I am so grateful to be who I am and where I am today. I truly believe that God was caring for me and developing me the entire time so I could know Him and be used by Him. I can now see just how God used all the events of my life to prepare me to handle being diagnosed with cancer. Without that difficult trial in my life, I would not have been able to write this book and share with you how great God is and how much He loves you and me.

Now, I find myself 30 years old, a husband to an amazing wife, and a father of two amazing little boys. I feel a lifetime away from that tumultuous year, and I struggle to believe I have just completed my eighth season in the NFL. My prayer for you as you read this book is that you too will take the time to look back on your life and see the many ways God has been at work in your life. May you have confidence that He has even more in store for you as His plan for your life continues to be revealed. God tells us in 1 Corinthians 10:13 that He will never give us more than we can bear. We will face challenges that seem impossible to handle while we are in the middle of them, but this Scripture rings true. We truly can get through anything if Jesus is the Lord of our lives!

Josh Bidwell's NFL Career Statistics

Year	Team	G	No.	Yds	Lg	Avg	Blk	I20	TB	Downed	No	Ret Yds	TD	Net Avg
1999	Green Bay Packers	0	0	0	0	—	0	0	0	0	0	0	0	—
2000	Green Bay Packers	16	78	3003	53	38.5	0	22	5	16	27	205	1	34.6
2001	Green Bay Packers	16	82	3485	68	42.5	0	21	10	14	34	288	0	36.5
2002	Green Bay Packers	16	79	3296	57	41.7	0	26	6	8	41	357	1	35.7
2003	Green Bay Packers	16	69	2875	60	41.7	0	16	7	13	32	316	0	35.1
2004	Tampa Bay Buccaneers	16	82	3472	60	42.3	0	23	7	17	31	279	0	36.8
2005	Tampa Bay Buccaneers	16	90	4101	61	45.6	0	24	13	10	49	466	0	37.5
2006	Tampa Bay Buccaneers	16	93	4045	59	43.5	0	20	7	11	50	487	1	36.8
TOTAL		112	573	24277	68	42.4	0	152	55	89	264	2398	3	36.2

KEY:

G	games played that year
No.	number of punts that year
Yds	cumulative yardage of all punts
Lg	longest punt of the season
Avg	average length of punt
Blk	number of punts blocked
I20	number of punts that left the opposing team inside their own 20
TB	touchbacks
Downed	punts that the receiver didn't catch
No	punts that the receiver caught but didn't make yardage on
Ret Yds	yards receivers returned punts
TD	punts returned for a touchdown
Net Avg	average distance on the play after the return

▼

To learn more about Josh Bidwell,

to invite him to speak to your organization,

or to find out how you can donate to his foundation,

visit his website at www.joshbidwell.com.

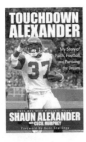

To learn more about Harvest House books
or to read sample chapters, log on to our website:

www.harvesthousepublishers.com

HARVEST HOUSE PUBLISHERS
EUGENE, OREGON